How to Succeed as a Freelance Translator

Corinne McKay

How to Succeed as a Freelance Translator
by Corinne McKay

ISBN 978-1-4116-9520-7
First Edition

Disclaimer: This book is published by Two Rat Press and Translatewrite, Inc., who acknowledge all trademarks. All information contained in this book is believed to be correct at the time of printing. However, readers are advised to seek professional advice where necessary, as the information in this book is based on the author's experiences. The author of this book is not professionally engaged in providing legal, financial or career planning advice. Please send comments or corrections to books@translatewrite.com.

For Dan, Ada and my parents, who sweeten
every day.

Contents

Introduction

I decided to write this book because I love my job, and because so few bilingual people are aware of the high demand for qualified translators and interpreters, or of the lifestyle benefits of being a language entrepreneur. In 2002, I was looking for a new career after eight years as a high school French teacher, and hoping to find a work-from-home job using my language skills. I thought back to a translation internship that I had done in college, and remembered how much I had enjoyed it. At the time, I had almost no knowledge of the translation industry nor any job contacts, so I started out by calling every company listed under *Translators and Interpreters* in the local yellow pages. Over the next few months I became involved with my local translators association, the American Translators Association (ATA), and began getting some calls for translation work. A year and some 400 résumés later, I passed the ATA certification exam in French to English translation, and my business continued to grow, while still allowing me to work from home on a flexible schedule, earning a healthy income and spending plenty of time with my family.

Although I spent most of that first year marketing my fledgling business, the effort paid off; after three years as a freelance translator I earned my highest gross income ever (including when I worked full-time as a teacher) while working 20–30 hours a week from home. I developed specializations in legal, financial and marketing translation, edited my local translators association newsletter, presented seminars at the annual conference of the American Translators Association and often found myself exclaiming, "This is *so* interesting!" while working on a translation—in short, I had found my niche.

At the same time, the path from that day with the phone book to the day I told a client, "Sorry, I'm booked for the next two weeks" was harder than it had to be, because there is a real shortage of training materials on how to run a translation business. Most translators enter the field because they love languages and writing, not because they love marketing and bookkeeping, but many translators' businesses fail because they lack basic business skills. If you'd like to succeed as a freelance translator, it's definitely important to pursue training in translation techniques, translation software, and other tools of the trade, but these types of courses are easier to locate. Part of the reason I decided to write this book was because, having never run my own business before, I struggled so much with these basic business questions: how and where to find prospective clients, how to pursue translator certification, how to decide whether expensive computer software would help my business, how to set my translation rates, and so on.

This book is based on the article *Getting Started as a Freelance Translator*, which first appeared on my website and was picked up by several translation websites. Later, I expanded that article into an online course that has continued to be very popular with aspiring translators. Following the success of the course, I realized that there must be many more people out there wondering how to use their language skills to break into the translation industry, and the idea for this book was born.

The good news about translation

If you're considering a career as a translator, there's a lot to look forward to. Given the global reach of businesses in the 21st century, translators are employed in almost every conceivable business sector, from banking to museums to health care to high-tech. If you have a special skill or interest in addition to being bilingual, you're almost sure to find clients who will pay for your services, and you'll get to work on materials that interest you. Overall, the United States Bureau of Labor Statistics http://bls.gov projects that job prospects for translators and interpreters will increase faster than the average until at least 2014. Translators are usually well paid for their work, with the most recent compensation survey by the American Translators Association reporting that the average self-employed full-time translator earns over $50,000 per year. Most translators, even if they work 40 hours a week or more, live a very self-directed lifestyle and can tailor their work day around other interests or commitments such as families.

The good news about virtual work

In publicizing their work-from-home newsletter *The Rat Race Rebellion*, the e-entrepreneurship specialists Staffcentrix `http://staffcentrix.com` estimate that "There is a 30 to 1 scam ratio among home-based work 'opportunities.' " Although there are definitely some unscrupulous translation clients out there, translation itself is a great example of a legitimate work-from-home opportunity. The vast majority of translators in the U.S. work from home, so translation agencies are used to this business model, and don't think it's odd to employ translators who work from home. Home work has a lot of advantages for you as the home worker, and for your community as a whole. By working from home, you'll probably experience greater job satisfaction and less stress, since a relatively minor disruption like a dentist appointment or furnace repair won't derail your entire work day. Most of the time, you'll be able to structure your work day around your peak energy times and your family's needs, rather than your employer's policies. Your commute will be as long as it takes you to walk from your bedroom to your office and fire up the computer while still in your pajamas. Not surprisingly, most home workers experience a greatly improved quality of life.

Likewise, working from home often has a very positive effect on your community and the world as a whole. Less commuting means less traffic congestion, less fuel usage and less need for parking areas. Home-based workers are around during the day, allowing them to volunteer for school and community activities and to be available for their families. A study by the International Telework Association and Council (ITAC) found that home-based workers are absent from work less than half as often as office-based workers, leading to greater work productivity in general.

Is freelance translation for you?

Despite all of these positive reports, it's very important to do some realistic self-assessment to determine if a career as a freelance translator is for you. Translators need a lot of skills besides fluency in at least two languages; translators need to be excellent writers in their native language and need to be interested in and skilled at terminology research using both paper dictionaries and the Internet. Translators also need to be avid readers in their native and non-native languages in order to keep up their language skills and their knowledge of world events.

Equally important, and the subject that we'll focus on in this book, is a translator's ability to run a business. When you work full-time for an employer, you have one job title. When you work for yourself, you're not only the translator, but also the department head for sales and marketing, technical support, customer relations, accounting and facilities maintenance. Unless you're willing and able to pay someone to do these tasks for you, you'll be doing them yourself, in addition to your regular job.

Before you launch yourself into a translation career, it's important to ask yourself a few questions. Are you the type of person who is often described as highly motivated, driven, a go-getter; or do you have trouble following through on a plan once the exciting idea stage is over? Are you consistently able to meet deadlines with almost no supervision or direction, or do you head off to shopping websites as soon as the boss disappears? Do you have the multi-tasking skills necessary to manage multiple clients and deadlines at once, or does this type of work leave you feeling overwhelmed and wondering where to start?

In addition, it's important to factor in a start-up period of at least six months to a year when launching your freelance business. Of course this is just an estimate, and the length of everyone's startup period will vary, but for translators who work in a relatively common language pair (for example French, Italian, German, Spanish or Portuguese paired with English), it's best to budget on at least six months of doing a lot of marketing and working less than full-time. For some people, for example parents of small children or full-time students who are looking for some supplemental income, the spotty cash flow of a startup period may not be a huge concern. If you're planning on translation as your full-time income, you'll need to either continue your current employment while your translation business gets up to speed, or plan on living off your savings or a loan during this time. It can help to focus on the fact that with a consistent and reasonably aggressive marketing effort, you'll have years to enjoy your freelance lifestyle and income after your startup phase ends.

So to all of you out there wondering, "What exactly does someone with a degree in foreign languages *do* for a living?," I wish you happy reading, and hopefully, happy translating!

Acknowledgments

Very few books are truly solo endeavors, and this book is no exception. Special thanks go to the people who lent their enthusiasm to this project when it was just an idea to toss around over coffee or e-mail: Eve Lindemuth Bodeux, Beth Hayden, Thomas Hedden, Bruce McKay, LaNelle McKay and Karen Mitchell for their insights and encouragement, and the students in the first two sessions of my course, *Getting Started as a Freelance Translator* for their excellent feedback on the course materials that this book is based on. My colleagues in the Colorado Translators Association, the American Translators Association and Boulder Media Women, and the readers of my e-newsletter *Open Source Update* are an ongoing source of knowledge and inspiration that every translator and writer should be so fortunate as to have. And Dan Urist... where to start... spent more hours than a recovering computer systems administrator should have to on the layout, design and editing of this book, learning at least two new pieces of software in the process and lovingly hounding me until the last word was written.

1 An overview of the translation business

1.1 What is a translator?

In a nutshell, a translator is a human being who changes written words from one language to another. If this sounds obvious, take another look! First, it's important to note that although computers play an important role in translation, professional translators are humans, not computers. Second, a translator works with written words, unlike an interpreter, who works with spoken words. If you're new to the industry, you've learned something important right here; that the phrase "speaking through a translator," contradicts itself, since translators work in writing. While some people work as both translators and interpreters, most concentrate on one or the other.

Translators are also, by definition, fluent in more than one language. In the industry, these are referred to as the *source*, or "from" language(s), and the *target*, or "into" language, which is almost always the translator's native language. So for example, a translator who is a native English speaker and learned Portuguese and Spanish might translate from Spanish and Portuguese into English. If you work in the most common language pairs, such as English paired with French, Italian, German or Spanish (known as FIGS in the translation industry), chances are that you will never translate into your second or third language. If you work in a less common language pair, you might find yourself as the exception to this rule. A client might need a document translated from Thai into English, a job that would usually be handled by a native English speaker who has Thai as a second or third language. However in practice, it's often easier to find a native Thai (or

Lingala, Malayalam, Fulani, etc) speaker who has English as a second language since there are many more native Thai speakers who also speak English than the other way around. In this case, the job might be handled by a native Thai speaker, and then proofread by a native English speaker.

In the United States, most translators work from one or two source languages; it's extremely common for translators to have only one working language pair, like Spanish into English, or Japanese into English. In other areas of the world where foreign languages are more widely studied, most translators work from at least two source languages, and often many more. It's not at all unusual to find Europe-based translators who work, for example, from English, Spanish and French into German, or from Norwegian, Swedish and English into Danish.

1.2 What does it take to become a translator?

Being multilingual isn't the only skill a translator needs, but it's certainly the most important. Translators learn their languages in many different ways; many grew up in bilingual households or countries, some learned their second or third language in school and then pursued experience abroad, some took intensive language courses or worked in a foreign country for several years, and it is also quite common for translators to become freelancers after working as military or government linguists. Almost all translators working in the U.S. have at least a Bachelor's Degree, although not necessarily in translation. As a rule, most professional translators have at least some experience working and/or living in a country where their source language or languages are spoken; many translators lived and worked in their source language country for many years, or pursued higher education in their source language(s). In-country experience is a big asset for a translator, since translation work involves knowing not just the structure of the language to be translated, but the cultural framework that surrounds it. This isn't to say that classroom study doesn't produce excellent translators, but it's important to realize at the outset that to be a successful professional translator, you need *near-native* proficiency in your source language(s); if you're starting from scratch, a few semesters of part-time language class won't be enough. As a point of reference, the U.S. Government's Defense Language Institute Foreign Language Center offers a program to teach Middle Eastern languages to government employees, and the *basic* program involves 63 weeks of full-time study.

Many people wonder how to tell if their language skills are good enough to work as a translator. While there are various language testing services that can tell you where you stand, probably the easiest way to get a feel for your translation readiness is to translate something. Go on the web and find a legal document, newspaper article or press release in your source language, then try to translate it. As we'll discuss later, professional translators make constant use of reference materials such as print and online dictionaries, terminology databases, etc., so when you look at your practice document, don't assume that you should be able to whip out a perfect translation on the spot. The key points are: can you understand this document on both a word-for-word and a conceptual level, and can you convey its meaning in your target language?

Translators today work in almost every conceivable language pair; while the market in the United States has historically been very strong in Western European languages such as French, German, Italian and Spanish, there is an increasing (and increasingly lucrative) market for translation in Asian and Middle Eastern Languages like Hindi, Gujarati, Urdu, Thai, Chinese, Japanese, Korean, Arabic, Farsi, Pashto and Kurdish; Central and Eastern European languages like Serbian, Czech, Slovene and Macedonian; as well as the "languages of smaller diffusion" like Nepali, Hebrew or Somali. In most language pairs, the amount of work available is proportionate to the number of translators in the language. While there is obviously a great deal of English to Spanish translation work in the U.S., there is a correspondingly large number of translators in this language combination; and while there may not be a great deal of work in Indonesian to English, there are also not many translators in this combination, resulting in a correspondingly small amount of competition for work.

In addition to near-native source language proficiency, translators need other skills too; probably the most important are excellent writing skills in their target language, in-depth knowledge in one or more areas of specialization, and business management skills. Some would-be translators are in practice not very successful because they have weak writing skills in their target language, making their translations difficult or unpleasant to read. Highly specialized translators are among the highest-earning members of the profession; for example a bilingual intellectual property attorney, stock broker or biomedical engineer may earn many times the per-word rate of a "jack of all trades" translator with a B.A. in German. Some translators turn a previous career into an area of specialization, while others take additional courses in areas of specialization or learn specialized terminology from more experienced translators. Paradoxically, specializing can also lead to more work, not less, as the specialized translator becomes known as the go-to person in his or her area of expertise, whether it's environmental engineering, textile manufacturing or stage sets.

The translation industry in the United States is moving more and more toward an independent contractor model, where the vast majority of translators are self-employed and work for a variety of clients; in 2005, approximately 70% of the members of the American Translators Association were self-employed independent contractors. As such, translators need business management skills such as the ability to find and retain clients, work on tight deadlines with little supervision or management, handle increases and decreases in work flow and cash flow and perform tasks such as bookkeeping, tax planning and computer upkeep and maintenance. In fact, most self-employed translators spend 25–50% of their time on non-translation work, largely involving management of the day to day tasks of running a business, so these skills are just as important as translation-related skills in succeeding as a freelance translator.

1.3 Improving your language skills

If you'd like to work as a translator but your language skills are not yet up to par, you have a few options. The best, but most difficult, is immersion: living and working or going to school in a country where your source language is spoken. If you want to improve your French, without a doubt the fastest way to do it is to move to a French-speaking country for a year, work or go to school with native French speakers, and speak only French while you're there. If this isn't possible for you, university programs in translation and interpretation do exist in the U.S., although they are much less common than in other countries. However, nearly all medium or large colleges and universities will offer advanced courses in the more widely spoken foreign languages. The American Translators Association http://atanet.org sells several publications listing translating and interpreting programs, and also has a mentoring program for its members, although the program is geared toward professional, not linguistic, development. If you're trying to improve your language skills, be realistic; although it's certainly far from impossible to learn a new language at age 30, 50 or 70, it's also not going to happen with a few semesters of night classes. If you're starting from a beginner level or close to it, two to three years of intensive language study in a college-level program is probably a bare minimum. However, if you have a solid foundation in a second or third language, for instance you studied it in school for 10 years including several trips to a country where the language is spoken, you might be ready to start translating right away.

As mentioned before, simply knowing more than one language isn't enough to guarantee your success as a translator. While requirements for different translation jobs vary, nearly all translators have at least a Bachelor's degree, and often more education than this. If you would eventually like to earn certification from the American Translators Association, you'll need either a Master's degree or higher, or several years of work experience as a translator. The rapid expansion of the translation industry, flexible work possibilities and high earning potential have made freelance translation an attractive career for bilingual lawyers, accountants, doctors and scientific professionals, and many translators feel that specialization is extremely important to their success. This is especially true as the Internet has opened up work opportunities for translators who live in countries where the cost of living is relatively low, and where educated professionals may be able to make more money by working as translators over the Internet than by practicing in the professions they were trained for.

1.4 A translator's working environment

The translation industry in the United States is moving more and more toward the independent contractor model. In the past, many large companies and even many translation agencies had staffs of in-house translators, but these jobs are now few and far between, and when they do exist would rarely be given to a beginner. In contrast to other professions where newcomers are expected to pay their dues as in-house employees and then enjoy the "reward" of freelancing, the translation industry usually works in the opposite way. Most translators start out as freelancers and may even remain self-employed for their whole careers, while most well-paid in-house translators are hired with years or even decades of experience. It's important to be realistic about whether the life of a freelancer is for you. While you'll have a great degree of control over where, when and how much you work, you'll also give up the security of a steady paycheck, benefits, paid time off, and a pension or employer-sponsored 401K.

Most freelance translators in the U.S. work from a home office, and there is no stigma attached to working from home; translators who rent office space outside the home are definitely the exception rather than the rule. The vast majority of a translator's work is done on the computer, using either a word processing program or text editor, and possibly a computer-assisted translation program. Translators make extensive use of reference materials such as print and online dictionaries, terminology databases, and discussion with other translators. The almost constant use of a computer makes repetitive strain injury one of the few work-related injuries that translators are at risk for.

There are many positive sides to a translator's work environment. Compared to other work-from-home jobs, translation can be very interesting and well-paying. Although you probably won't get lavishly rich working as a freelance translator, translation industry compensation surveys report that the average self-employed freelance translator earns about $52,000 per year. Translators who are highly specialized in technical fields, or work with in-demand language pairs may earn much more than this, and in-house translators for certain branches of the U.S. government or international financial institutions may earn $70,000 a year and up.

At the same time, it is important to be realistic about the time and effort involved in reaching this level of income. Unless you work in a language pair and/or specialization that is extremely in demand, it may take a year or more to develop a regular client base that will allow you to replace the income from a previous full-time job, and you will probably need to send out several hundred résumés during that time. Before starting your freelance translation business, it's important to determine if you have the financial resources, time and energy to get through the startup period to the point where you are earning a reasonable and steady income.

Starting a translation business is a fairly inexpensive proposition. If you already have a home computer and high speed Internet access, you might make do with business cards, computerized fax service and a modest reference library, for a startup cost of only a few hundred dollars. To a large extent, freelancers can determine when and how much they want to work. While it probably makes good business sense to accept as much work as possible from your regular clients, on a day-to-day basis many translators work on their own schedule rather than from 9 to 5. A translator's eight hour day might run from 7:30–11:30 AM and 4:30–8:30 PM. This flexibility makes translation an excellent career option for people who have young children, are semi-retired, or just want to work part-time. Today, most translation work happens remotely, and translators can live almost anywhere. The up and down nature of most freelancers' work loads also lends itself to using free time to take classes, pursue hobbies, travel or spend time with family.

On the downside (and of course there are some downsides to all of this!), as with other consulting or freelance work, some aspects of translation can be stressful and difficult to manage. Many translators describe their work as feast or famine, with months of little work and months of working every waking moment and more than a few moments that should be spent sleeping. Worldwide business acceleration has affected translation turnaround times, with agencies eager to have translations returned as soon as possible, sometimes within a few hours for a short project. Clients who pay late or don't pay at all can cause major financial problems, especially for translators who live paycheck to paycheck. Translators who work in common language combinations like Spanish↔English may face pressure to lower their rates in order to remain competitive, especially if the client can find qualified translators in countries where pay rates are much lower. In addition, working from home has its ups and downs; even for an introvert, the life of the home office can be lonely, and time spent on (unpaid) non-translation work like accounting, marketing and maintaining computer systems can become frustrating when you'd much rather be translating! If you've never worked for yourself before, succeeding as a translator demands a high degree of self-discipline. With no boss in the next cubicle and a list of household errands to finish, it can be hard to focus on your work, and if you have a family or housemates, equally difficult to find a work-friendly time and space in your house.

However, most translators enjoy their work and like to talk about what they do and how they got started. The ever-changing nature of the job appeals to many people, since no day "at the office" is exactly like another. Another positive aspect of the job is that most translation clients value their translators and treat them as professionals who deserve to be fairly paid for their work. Even in the most common language combinations, the supply of qualified and capable (emphasis here!) translators often cannot keep pace with the industry's demand, resulting in a generally positive employment picture for translators and interpreters. The United States Bureau of Labor Statistics reports that employment prospects for translators and interpreters should grow faster than the average for all occupations until at least 2014.

1.5 What kinds of work do translators do?

As cross-cultural and multilingual communication become more important to the worldwide flow of business, translators and interpreters are employed in almost every conceivable business and government sector. From law to health care to finance, entertainment, information technology and advertising, translators and interpreters enable global communication. Some translators, especially those with specialized professional or technical training, might concentrate on only one subject area, such as pharmaceuticals, corporate finance, computer software or legal contracts. There are even translators who specialize in seemingly obscure areas like fisheries management, shopping mall construction, stamps, or groundwater hydrology. Still others position themselves as "jack of all trades" translators with concentrations in certain areas. In general, the more translators there are in a given language pair, the more specialization is required, and the smaller the translator pool, the less incentive there is to specialize. German to English translators in the U.S. almost certainly have specializations, but the same isn't necessarily true of the few Bosnian to English translators doing business in the same markets.

Translators sometimes work in collaboration with other linguists, particularly if the work involves a large project that needs to be translated in a short amount of time. Today, translation teams almost always work together over the Internet, rather than in person. The size of translation projects can vary widely, from a single line of text such as a company slogan, to an entire book or website. Most translators who are self-employed work from project to project, with the average project taking anywhere from an hour to several days, and some longer projects mixed in as well. Most translators working in the United States today work on business and technical documents, rather than literature.

Although most translators in the U.S. are independent contractors, full-time jobs for translators and interpreters do exist, particularly in areas such as court and health care interpreting, web content translation, software localization, and translating and interpreting for the United States Government's various agencies including the Federal Bureau of Investigation, Central Intelligence Agency and National Security Agency. Translators who are experienced and/or qualified to work in more than one language pair may have a greater chance of being offered an in-house position.

Literary translators (translators who work on books, poetry or short stories) make up a relatively small segment of translators in the United States. This is because literary translation is typically not very well paid, and because Americans don't tend to read literature in translation, so there is a small market for the work of literary translators; in 2004, only 891 of the 195,000 new books printed in English were adult literature in translation. If you translate into a language other than English, there may be a larger market for literary translation services, especially if you are qualified to work on textbooks, technical manuals, and other "non-literary" book projects.

Localization translators are a rapidly growing group in the industry. Localization, or the complete adaptation of a product such as a web site, product marketing kit, software program or advertising campaign into another language, used to be confined mostly to computer software. Now, software localization is probably the largest segment of the localization market, but it's certainly not the only segment. Businesses may hire localization agencies when they want to take a new product global and need culturally-targeted marketing advice in addition to translation services.

1.5.1 Software Localization

A sub-specialty within the translation and localization industry is software localization, the process of translating software user interfaces from one language to another. For example, when a large software company produces multilingual versions of its applications, every piece of text displayed by the software must be translated into the target language, and in many cases the graphics must be altered as well. Software localization involves both bilingual software developers and document translators specialized in information technology, since the software's user interface, help files, readme files, screen shots and incidental files (such as warranty information and packaging) must all be translated.

Software localization is an enormous industry in its own right, largely because computer users throughout the world now expect their software to be in their own language, and will naturally be more interested in purchasing software or visiting websites that they can access in their own language. Therefore, the software localization industry is a source of a large amount of work for bilingual software developers and for translators, and is currently one of the fastest-growing sectors within the translation industry as a whole. In addition, localization breeds localization; a localized web browser automatically creates a need for localized websites; a localized piece of software demands a localized manual to go with it. Two useful resources for localization professionals are the Globalization and Localization Association `http://www.gala-global.org` and the Localization Industry Standards Association `http://www.lisa.org`. Software localization is often completed using different tools than those that are used for document translation; some computer-assisted translation tools can cross over between these two types of translation, and some cannot. So, it is important to investigate what tools will be required if you would like to look for software localization work.

1.6 Who do translators work for?

1.6.1 Working for translation agencies

For a freelance translator, there are typically two types of clients: translation agencies and direct clients. First, let's look at how translators work through agencies. A translation agency, which may also refer to itself as a localization agency, translation company, or translation bureau, has its own roster of clients and sub-contracts their translation work to individual freelance translators. The agency handles the project management end of things, interacts directly with the translation client and (hopefully) pays the translator and deals with any collections issues. Ideally, the translation agency should pay its freelance translators when their invoices come due (normally 30 days after the agency accepts the translation) whether the agency itself has been paid by the end client or not.

A translation agency is not an employment agency, and there is no fee involved for a translator to register with an agency. However, an agency normally cannot guarantee a steady flow of work to any one translator, and will normally pay the translator a good deal less than the per-word rate that the agency is charging the client, in many cases up to 50% less. Freelance translators are often required to sign a confidentiality and non-competition agreement which states that they may not work directly for any of the agency's clients for some period of time, or may not disclose who the agency's clients are, or the nature of the assignments that they work on. Like translators themselves, translation agencies can be either very general, "all languages, all subjects," or highly specialized, for instance translating only for the medical industry, or only translating between English and Korean.

In the uncertain world of freelancing, translation agencies provide some measure of job security. When you work for an agency, you don't normally have to communicate with the end client directly, and in many cases the agency may even forbid you from contacting the end client. Instead, you translate the documents that the agency sends you, which means that you spend your time working instead of managing the project and handling the client's questions. Also, an agency that becomes a regular client may be able to provide you with steady work, and will often pay you even if the client is late in paying them. A good agency project manager understands the nature of translation work, and asks the client in advance to clarify potential questions, for example should currency amounts in Euros be converted to dollars, saving the contract translators a great deal of time. Many of the best agency project managers are or have been translators themselves. Agencies also provide some amount of "disaster insurance" in the event that you get sick in the middle of the project, suddenly find yourself in over your head on a very technical document, or another type of unforeseen event. If something like this happens, the agency can often find a replacement translator or editor to step in, which is a responsibility that falls upon the translator if an agency is not involved.

In exchange for the services the agency provides, you will give up some freedom. The agencies you work for may have fixed pay rates, or may ask you to reduce your rates to stay competitive with other translators. When an agency becomes a regular client, you want to keep them happy, so it will be hard to say "No!" when they call you on Friday afternoon with a big project due Monday, disrupting your planned ski trip or home improvement project. Also, agencies vary in quality. While a good agency can effectively hand you work on a platter and deal with all problems that come up between them and the end client, in practice this doesn't always happen. An agency may claim (rightly or wrongly) that you did a substandard job on a project for them, and then ask for or just go ahead and take a "discount" on the payment you agreed on. Or, an agency may not have much cash in reserve, and might not be able to pay you if the end client doesn't pay them. Agencies also have their own set payment terms, and in most cases the terms aren't negotiable. For example, agencies in the U.S. generally pay within 30 days from the date of the invoice (referred to as *Net 30*), or 30 days from the end of the month (*30 Days EOM*), while agencies in Europe take longer to pay, sometimes as long as 60 days from the end of the month or

90 days from the date of the invoice.

1.6.2 Working for direct clients

The other main option for a freelancer is to work for direct clients, meaning working directly for translation customers without a "middleman" involved. A direct client might be a shoe manufacturer in Sweden that wants to market its products in the U.S., a patent law firm in Japan, a university in the U.S. with non-English speaking visitors, or an individual who wants her high school diploma translated into French so that she can study abroad. The income potential of working for direct clients is attractive; in many cases double the income of working for an agency. Direct clients may also be able to provide large volumes of work if their turnaround time allows for it. Whereas a translation agency will often split a large project between several translators to get it done faster, a direct client might be willing to let you translate their entire 50,000 word annual report, resulting in more income and less administrative overhead for you; or they might be willing to let you act as a "mini-agency," subcontracting work to other translators you know and keeping a percentage for yourself. With a direct client the translator is often more in control of the payment terms involved; for example, the translator might be able to request payment in advance for certain services, an option that almost never exists when working through a translation agency.

There are some disadvantages in working for direct clients as well. When you work through an agency, it's the project manager's job to explain the ins and outs of the translation process to the client. If the client doesn't know what source and target language mean, or the difference between traditional and simplified Chinese, or whether they want the company's name in all capital letters throughout the document, it's the agency's responsibility to deal with this, not yours. When you work for a direct client, for better or worse there's no one between you and the client. In cases involving a small project such as a birth certificate translation, it might take more time to explain the process to the client than it does to complete the translation. If the client has an unrealistic deadline, keeps changing his/her mind about the project specifications, or wants additional services such as desktop publishing, it's up to you as the translator to deal with it. If the direct client doesn't pay, there's no one else to lean on for the money—you simply have to handle it yourself, or hire a collection agency if things turn really sour. All of these aspects are worth considering before you decide whether to work through agencies or for direct clients.

Somewhere between an agency and a direct client is a small but growing group of freelance project managers. These individuals function somewhat like one-person translation agencies, and may be handling outsourced translation for a larger corporation. This style of business combines some of the advantages and disadvantages of the agency/direct client model. Probably the most significant item to discuss up front is what happens if the end client doesn't pay or is late in paying the project manager who hires you, since unlike a large translation agency, this individual probably doesn't have the cash reserves to cover a large bill that goes unpaid.

1.7 A bit about interpreting

As you explore a career in translation, it's worth considering whether you would like to focus your business exclusively on translation, or include interpreting in your range of services. Like translation, the market for interpreting depends largely on your language pair(s), and unless you do over the phone interpreting, is more location-dependent than translation since you need to be in the same place as your clients.

Interpreting has several "modes," the primary ones being simultaneous, where the interpreter talks at the same time as the speaker; consecutive, where the interpreter listens to the speaker and takes notes, then interprets what the speaker said; and sight translation, where the interpreter reads a written document in another language, for example taking a court document in English and reading it to a defendant in Spanish. Simultaneous interpreting is probably the most common mode, since it is used at the United Nations, in court, and in various other conference-type settings.

Interpreting demands very different skills than translation. While translators are stereotypically detail-oriented introverts who don't mind spending an hour finding the perfect translation for a word, interpreters must be able to think on their feet and work with little or no advance preparation. Translators most often work alone at home, while interpreters are often literally in the spotlight, standing next to a court witness, hospital patient or head of state and communicating for him or her.

Until the advent of conference calling, interpreters had to be in the same place as their clients, and court and conference interpreting is still heavily dependent on on-site interpreters. However, over-the-phone interpreting is becoming more popular, especially in areas where it's hard to find on-site interpreters. Many translation agencies also schedule interpreters, and courts, hospitals and schools may employ in-house interpreters.

One major difference between interpreting and translation is that interpreters often work in both "directions" of their language pair, so must be highly proficient in speaking their non-native language; many high-level conference interpreters consider themselves to have two native languages, rather than one native language and one or more second languages. Interpreters are paid by the hour or by the day, and pay varies widely. In some areas of the U.S., English↔Spanish court interpreters might make less than $15 an hour, while conference interpreters who are members of the elite AIIC (International Association of Conference Interpreters) might make close to $500 a day.

If you are interested in interpreting, one excellent way to assess your skills is to go spend a day as an observer in court. Most courts in the U.S. are open to the public, and you can sit in the viewing area and try to interpret as the proceedings go along; better yet take a notebook and make a list of words and expressions that you need to research. The major employers of interpreters in the U.S. are courts, health care settings and schools, so these are all good places to focus on if you would like to explore interpreting.

1.8 How do translators set their rates?

Translators are generally paid by the word, with some variation in whether the word count is based on the source or target language, for a single word (most common in the U.S.) or per thousand words (most common in the U.K.), although payment is sometimes made by the line as well, with a line being comprised of a certain number of characters. For projects where charging by the word would result in a ridiculously low payment, for example translating an advertising slogan, translators are often paid by the hour. Translations of official documents such as birth certificates may be billed by the page. Many translators have a minimum charge for small projects, for example a flat fee for projects up to 250 words. It's also common for translators to add a premium for a rush project, or to offer a discount for a large project or ongoing work.

The actual per-word rate depends on your language combination(s) and specialization(s), and also on what your clients are willing to pay. Asking "How much do translators charge?" is like asking, "How big is a ball of yarn?" The variation in translation rates is enormous; if you visit online translation marketplaces such as Translators Cafe http://translatorscafe.com, or ProZ.com http://proz.com, you'll see an abundance of translators willing to work for just a few cents a word, while a highly specialized medical, legal or technical translator working for direct clients might make mid-double digits (cents, not dollars!) per word. In addition, many translators are reluctant to publish or even discuss their rates for fear of being targeted by antitrust actions.

If you work for translation agencies, there may not be much room for negotiation on rates, and "setting your rates" may be more a matter of finding agencies that are willing to pay what you would like to earn. Agencies will often ask you what your rates are, but just as often the agency already knows what it can or will pay for a typical project in your language combination, and is unlikely to give you work if you charge more than the "standard" rate. Some agencies will also tell you up front that you're welcome to specify your rates, but that the agency prefers to work with translators who charge less than a certain number of cents per word. Still, translation agencies as a group are not usually out to get translators to work for an absolute rock-bottom price, and will usually offer a fair rate for a project. Reputable agencies may even look askance at translation rates that are more than about 10% below the average or standard rate in a certain language combination.

1.9 Professional Associations for Translators and Interpreters

Professional associations are an excellent resource for both begin-ning and experienced translators and interpreters. At the interna-tional, national, and local levels, professional associations allow you to network with colleagues, pursue continuing education workshops and attend conferences related to the field. They also improve your credibility as a linguist. As one agency manager comments, "If a person is a member of a professional association, it shows that he or she has a network of colleagues to draw on and is willing to invest some time and money in the profession." Especially if translator or interpreter certification isn't offered in your languages, belonging to a professional association shows that you're serious about your work. Following is an overview of professional associations for translators and interpreters working in the United States.

1.9.1 American Translators Association

The American Translators Association http://atanet.org is the largest professional association for language professionals in the U.S., and offers membership to both individual linguists and translation companies. The Association also includes various language or specialization-specific divisions that members can choose to join. Benefits for ATA members include a listing on the ATA website, a subscription to the monthly magazine *ATA*

Chronicle, reduced rates to attend ATA conferences and seminars, and various professional benefits such as credit card acceptance, retirement programs, etc. The ATA holds a large annual conference each year in the fall, and information about upcoming conferences is also available on the ATA website.

The ATA administers its own certification exams, which are probably the most widely recognized translation credential in the U.S. As of 2006, candidates for the certification exam must also be members of ATA. For more information on certification exam dates, see ATA's website. 2006 individual dues are $145 per year.

1.9.2 National Association of Judiciary Interpreters and Translators

The National Association of Judiciary Intrpreters and Translators `http://najit.org` is a professional association for court interpreters and legal translators. NAJIT holds an annual conference, publishes the newsletter *Proteus*, and advocates for positive changes in the court interpreting and legal translation professions. NAJIT's website also includes a helpful list of Frequently Asked Questions (FAQ) about court interpreting. 2006 individual dues are $105 per year.

1.9.3 Translators and Interpreters Guild

The Translators and Interpreters Guild `http://ttig.org` is the only national (U.S.) union of translators and interpreters, operating as Local 32100 of the Newspaper Guild–Communications Workers of America. The Translators and Interpreters Guild operates a translator referral service that is open to members, and offers additional membership benefits such as a union credit card, life insurance, and legal services. 2006 individual dues are $120 per year.

1.9.4 American Literary Translators Association

The American Literary Translators Association `http://literarytranslators.org` is dedicated to serving literary translators and "enhancing the status and quality of literary translation." Members receive a variety of publications about literary translation, such as *Translation Review* and ALTA *Guides to Literary Translation*, and ALTA also holds an annual conference on literary translation. 2006 individual dues are $65 per year.

1.9.5 Fédération Internationale des Traducteurs

The Federation International des Traducteurs `http://fit-ift.org` is an "association of associations" for translators, which gathers more than 100 professional associations for language professionals from all over the world. FIT does not accept individual translators as members, but does hold an annual conference open to translators and interpreters throughout the world.

1.9.6 International Association of Conference Interpreters

Membership in AIIC `http://aiic.net` is open only to experienced conference interpreters who have worked a minimum of 150 days in a conference setting, and must be sponsored by three active AIIC members who have been in the association for at least five years. The AIIC website contains many helpful articles and links for aspiring and experienced interpreters.

1.10 Certification for Translators

As we discussed in a previous section, for better or worse, you don't have to have any type of certification to call yourself a translator or interpreter in the United States. Various organizations offer certification, but the list of language combinations is far from comprehensive. For example, organizations in the United States offer certification only in language combinations that involve English, so if you translate or interpret German into French or Japanese into Korean, there simply is no certification available in the U.S.. Reliable and uniform certification is one of the most

important issues facing the translation and interpreting professions today. Since no standardized certification for translators
and interpreters exists, there is little agreement on what makes
a "certified" translator or interpreter. In some cases, linguists
who have earned a certificate in translation or interpreting refer
to themselves as "certified," while to others, "certified" means
having passed a nationally standardized examination.

There is a great deal of controversy over whether certification is
a reasonable guarantee of a quality job, or whether non-certified
translators and interpreters are to be avoided. As a linguist,
especially in a common language combination such as English
with French, Spanish or German, becoming certified is one way
to distinguish yourself from the pack of questionably qualified
people offering translation or interpreting services in these languages, and certification may be required for certain types of
work. In some court systems it is now difficult to find work as
an English↔Spanish court interpreter if you're not certified, and
some translation agencies may insist that for certain end clients or
certain types of translations, you have to be certified if the option
is available for your languages. In addition, the American Translators Association's most recent compensation survey (published in
January, 2006), found that certified translators earn approximately
$6,000 per year more than their non-certified colleagues.

On the downside, there are numerous translators and interpreters with excellent qualifications who have failed certification
exams, or don't feel that they want to take them at all. As one
translation agency manager comments, "Certification doesn't
mean that the person can meet a deadline, work well with other
translators or respond to client input and questions, and all of
these are crucial to winning and keeping clients." More practically,
the certification exam itself represents a somewhat artificial environment in which you're asked to demonstrate your skills. For
instance, although the ATA is currently pursuing the possibility
of offering computerized certification exams, the exam currently
must be handwritten, something a practicing translator would
seldom if ever do. Hopefully, the computerized ATA certification
exam will become a reality in the near future.

Following is an overview of the main certifying organizations for translators and interpreters in the United States. If you work in a language combination that doesn't involve English, an Internet search can help you find certifying organizations in a country where your languages are spoken.

1.10.1 American Translators Association

The American Translators Association `http://atanet.org` offers *certification* (formerly called *accreditation*) to translators in 27 language pairs as of 2006; passing the exam earns you the right to add the designation "ATA-certified for X to X translation" to your credentials. As of this writing, the available certifications are (↔ indicates that the test is available in either "direction"):

- Arabic→English

- Danish→English

- English→Chinese

- Croatian↔English

- Dutch↔English

- French↔English

- German↔English

- Hungarian↔English

- Italian↔English

- Japanese↔English

- Polish↔English

- Portuguese↔English

- Russian↔English

- Spanish↔English

As of January, 2004, candidates for the ATA certification exam must also fulfill an education and experience requirement before being allowed to sit for the exam. To fulfill this requirement, you must meet one of the following criteria:

- Certification or accreditation by an organization that is a member of the Fédération Internationale des Traducteurs.

- A degree or certificate from an approved Translation and Interpreting program (see ATA website for list of approved programs) or a Master's degree, PhD or equivalent degree in any field.

- A Bachelor's degree and two years' experience working as a translator or interpreter (see ATA website for how to demonstrate your work experience).

- Less than a Bachelor's degree and five years' experience working as a translator or interpreter (see ATA website for how to demonstrate your work experience).

While all of this sounds intimidating and does exclude many people who previously could have taken the exam, it's important to remember that if you already have a Master's degree or PhD in any subject area, you meet the requirement. If you don't have an advanced degree, probably the fastest way to gain eligibility is to earn a certificate from an approved translation or interpreting program, but this depends on your financial resources and the availability of a school near you.

1.10.2 Federal Court Interpreter Certification Examination Program

The Federal Court Interpreter Certification Examination Program http://cps.ca.gov/fcice-spanish/index.asp is perhaps the most widely recognized credential for interpreters in the United States. Passing this examination, most commonly offered in Spanish↔English but also in Navajo↔English and

Haitian Creole↔English, earns you the designation *Federally Certified Court Interpreter*. The examination is rigorous, necessitating that the candidate maintain simultaneous interpreting speeds of up to 160 words per minute, and retain passages of up to 50 words in length for consecutive interpreting. FCICE candidates must first pass a written test with a score of at least 75%, and are then invited to take the oral portion of the exam, on which a score of 80% is considered passing. At present, the oral portion consists of a sight translation, simultaneous interpretation, and mock cross-examination, involving both consecutive and simultaneous interpretation. The exam is offered on specific dates in specific locations specified on the program's website, so if you don't live near one of these cities, you'll have to travel there in order to take the exam.

A self-assessment of readiness to take the FCICE exam is included on the program website, and numerous preparation courses have sprung up in order to meet the growing demand especially for Spanish↔English court interpreters in certain areas of the United States. Other than the FCICE site itself, an excellent resource is Acebo, a language resources company run by highly qualified interpreter trainers. The Acebo website http://acebo.com has a section with "Tips for the Federal Exam," and also sells preparation materials for interpreting exams, the best known of which are *The Interpreter's Edge* and *The Interpreter's Edge Turbo Supplement*.

The advantage of having the Federally Certified Court Interpreter credential depends on where you live and what type of work you want to do. In areas of the U.S. with large Spanish-speaking populations, courts often have full-time staff interpreter positions, with standard pay for interpreters in the Federal courts set at approximately $330.00 per day. As the FCICE credential becomes more well-known, many interpreters report that private clients such as conference organizers and law firms are more likely to insist on using federally certified interpreters. Because of the rigorous nature of the federal certification examination, it is usually seen as a reliable indicator of a quality interpreter.

1.10.3 State Court Interpreter Certification

Court interpreter certification at the state level is much less standardized than at the federal level. Some states such as Washington, New Jersey, California and Colorado have active programs to certify court interpreters of Spanish and other languages as well, and strongly suggest that courts use only certified interpreters. Other states are moving toward this type of model, while still others have no certification procedures at all. The best source of information on what's available in your state is The Consortium for State Court Interpreter Certification `http://ncsconline.org/D_Research/CourtInterp.html`. The Consortium has developed interpreter certification tests in Spanish, Russian, Vietnamese, Korean, Hmong, Cantonese, Laotian, Haitian Creole, Arabic, Mandarin and Somali, with tests in progress (as of 2006) for Portuguese and Serbian. Whether these tests are offered in your state is another issue, but you can find this out by visiting the *Testing Schedule for 2006* link from the Consortium website.

The value of obtaining state certification depends again on where you live and what type of work you'd like to do. In states where certification is becoming better known, it may be difficult or impossible to find work as a court interpreter if you're not certified. In other states, certification may be almost unknown even by the people who hire court interpreters.

2 Starting and Growing your Freelance Translation Business

2.1 Preparing for your job search

Whether you're just starting out as a translator or moving from in-house to freelance work, finding your first clients is one of the biggest challenges you'll face. For most beginning translators, it will be hard to find well-paying work unless you have either a degree in translation or some translation experience. If you have both excellent language skills and work experience in a technical field, for example if you are a doctor and bilingual in Russian, it may be worth sending off your résumé even without translation experience. For the rest of us, it's important to compose a file of samples and references before applying to agencies or direct clients. Here are some ways to go about beefing up your résumé if you're starting from zero.

2.1.1 The basics of writing a translation résumé

Having a translation-targeted résumé is your most crucial first step in starting your job search. Since some translation agencies will look *only* at your résumé, it's especially important to have a strong one, as your cover letter may never be seen by the person responsible for delegating projects. If you are e-mailing your résumé, you should send it in either Microsoft Word format or as a PDF. Whatever the format of your résumé, it is absolutely imperative that it is well written and contains *no errors* in grammar or spelling. Remember, you are applying for language work—why would a potential client trust this work to someone whose own application materials don't show evidence of good language practices? Let's look at some important features of a well-written translator résumé.

2.1.2 A new résumé for a new career

As a beginning translator, the number one thing your résumé needs to do is convince a potential client to take a chance on you instead of giving the job to a more experienced linguist. Many beginning translators fail from the get-go because they use the same résumé that they've been sending out to look for a job in banking, health care, teaching or sales, wrongly assuming that they have nothing to write about their qualifications as a translator. If you are not familiar at all with writing a résumé, or with writing one for the U.S., large online job search sites such as Monster.com http://monster.com have extensive "career search help" sections that can help you get started and learn how to format your résumé. Even if you are familiar with how to write a strong résumé, spend some time on the Web looking at how other translators present themselves; online translation portals such as Translators Cafe http://translatorscafe.com and ProZ.com http://proz.com are good places to start.

The first step in the résumé reinvention process is to think about and research what your potential clients are looking for in a translator. Obviously they want someone who knows at least two languages, but on top of that, think about what your clients are seeking and what skills you can offer that you've already developed in your current career. For example, translators need to be able to work independently on tight deadlines without the oversight of a boss. Translators work on computers almost all the time, and need to know how to use computers efficiently. Translators also need excellent writing skills in their target language and excellent communications skills to work well with clients. Specialized translators need to know terminology in their areas of specialization. Some or all of these skills may be transferable from your current career. Therefore, it can be a good idea to start out your résumé-writing process by thinking about or even writing down the key career skills you've developed that will make you a good risk to a new client.

2.1.3 The structure of your résumé

This section will focus mainly on writing a résumé for use in the U.S.. However, it is a good idea to have résumés in both your source and target languages so that you can apply to translation agencies or direct clients in your non-native language countries. Make sure to follow good translation practice yourself and have the résumé in your non-native language proofread by a native speaker. Following are some factors to consider when preparing your résumé for use in the U.S. or abroad.

- A résumé for use in the U.S. is quite streamlined compared to what's expected in many other countries. It is generally only one page long, two pages at most, and does not include much personal information other than your name and contact information, including address, telephone number and email address. If you are going to be posting your résumé on the Internet, you might consider removing your physical address from that version of your résumé. A U.S. résumé can be organized either chronologically (usually starting with your current job and then going in reverse), or functionally (using categories such as **Professional Qualifications**, **Skills Summary** etc.). A résumé for the U.S. is *always* typeset (not hand written), and uses lots of active verbs, promoting the person's accomplishments: "established," "created," "managed," etc. A U.S. résumé, as compared with résumés for other countries, also tends to emphasize what the prospective employer will gain from hiring the candidate, rather than what the candidate would like to gain from the employer.

- A résumé for use in Europe contains much more personal information. It is common to list your date and place of birth, citizenship(s), marital status, and sometimes even number of children. A scanned photograph is also sometimes included. For a résumé intended for the U.S., note that this type of information should *never* be included on your U.S. résumé since it is actually illegal for employers to ask for it in most cases. If you send a European résumé through the mail, it is sometimes seen as a "plus" to send a hand written résumé and cover letter. Many European employers feel that a hand written résumé or cover letter lets them evaluate your language skills and may also be submitted for an analysis of your personal traits as revealed through your handwriting. On a European résumé, "chronological order" normally means reverse chronological order, so you would start with your first job and end with the one you have now. European résumés also tend to be less promotional in nature, and use more passive and descriptive language such as "responsibilities included..."

- An Asian résumé is much more comprehensive than a U.S. or even a European one. For example, while on a U.S. résumé you would seldom include levels of education below college or professional school unless you didn't attend these, on a résumé to be sent to Japan or China your **Education** section might include every school you attended starting with kindergarten, which would reveal insights into your family's socioeconomic status.

2.1.4 Your name

The first item on your résumé will be your name. Assuming you know your own name, this sounds laughably easy, but it isn't. Here are some observations on why it's necessary to give some thought to the name you use professionally, especially when you're dealing with multilingual and multicultural environments:

- You may want to clarify your gender. In your source language culture, your name may be gender indeterminate, making it awkward when potential clients don't know how to address you. If you want, you can solve this problem up front by identifying yourself somewhere on your application materials as "Fouad Tarkari (Mr.)" or "Ms. Poonam Prakash." Likewise, U.S.-based translators may want to do this when sending materials to their source language countries.

- Choose one name and spelling, and use it consistently. Especially if your name involves any transliteration, pick one version and stick to it. Going by different names can also present payment problems when the agency writes a check or tries to complete a wire transfer under a different spelling of your name.

2.1.5 Your summary of qualifications

This section, which goes below your name and contact information and might also be called an **Objective** and **Profile** section, is key to getting started as a translator. If the first item on your résumé is a detailed description of your ten years of work as an auto mechanic with no mention of language skills, clients may not even make it to the **Education** section to find out that you're actually bilingual in English and Japanese and interested in automotive translation; with a summary of qualifications you highlight this fact right away. A good way to research what qualifications your potential clients want is to read some translation agency websites; after all, you'll be delivering a good deal of the product that they're promising their clients. Including some of these desired characteristics is a good way to start your résumé on a positive note. Following are some sample summaries of qualifications for career changing translators.

For that Japanese→English auto mechanic:

Objective: Freelance Japanese to English translation assignments for companies in the automotive industry, using skills in the areas of project completion, quality assurance and communication, demonstrated by ten years of profitable self-employment in the automotive industry.

Profile: Native speaker of U.S. English, B.A. in Japanese including one year of residency in Japan. Excellent computer skills including office software and Internet research. Large collection of specialized bilingual dictionaries; recently completed online translator training course. Accustomed to meeting numerous deadlines per day and providing superior customer service.

For a bilingual nurse:

Objective: Freelance English<>Spanish medical translation work, making use of extensive experience and qualifications in the health care field including Spanish--English bilingual health care settings.

Profile: Fully bilingual registered nurse, grew up in Spanish--English bilingual household with numerous extended visits to Mexico. Registered nurse since 1995 including three years' experience providing primary care to limited English proficiency (LEP) Spanish-speaking patients. In-depth knowledge of Spanish and English medical terminology including confidential handling of medical records. Excellent written communications skills including chart and medical report writing.

2.1.6 The body of the résumé

Next, you'll have to decide whether to structure your résumé functionally or chronologically. If the type of translation work you're seeking is somewhat related to your current work, you might opt for a chronological résumé. For example if you're currently a lawyer and would like to do legal translation, your résumé can be structured fairly traditionally. If you're breaking off on a completely new path, for example if you've worked as a ski instructor for five years and would like to do website translation, you may opt for a functional résumé, which in the most extreme examples doesn't even include your job titles or where you've worked, just summaries of your skills and experience.

Below your summary of qualifications, for whichever style of résumé you choose, you should include sections for **Education** and **Professional Experience** or **Related Experience**; other than this the sections are up to you. For example, some translators like to include a **Skills and Interests** section in case potential clients have work in one of their avocational areas like sports, music, cooking, etc. The key here is to structure your résumé so that it draws attention to what you can offer, not what's missing. You should also include any professional credentials you have even if they're not translation related; for example if you're a certified public accountant, certified energy rater, licensed professional engineer, etc.

When you're writing your first translation-targeted résumé, you should highlight any experience you have, both in the areas of language and subject matter. If you studied abroad in Mexico in 1975, include it. If you belong to a local translators association, include it. If you recently attended a conference on estate and will terminology, include it. If you just taught a French class for elementary school students, include it. Obviously you can't fabricate résumé details, but if you're planning to make translation your full-time or only job, it is fair to refer to yourself as a "self-employed freelance translator" (including your language pairs) and describe the work you are doing now. As your translation experience grows (and it will!), change the format of your résumé to reflect this.

2.1.7 What about a cover letter?

Since most freelance translation work is conducted over the Internet, a formal cover letter really isn't necessary or even appropriate for most translators. The exception would be if you are interested in doing direct client work, in which case you might be sending your materials through the mail or by fax instead of over the Web. Most of the time, you will either send a short e-mail cover letter, or include a paragraph or two in the "Additional Information" field of a translation agency's online application.

Your e-mail cover letter should be short and to the point. Keep in mind that many translation agencies receive several thousand translator applications per year, and it's unlikely that whoever receives your e-mail will take the time to read the usual five-paragraph cover letter. Instead, pare down your message to the essentials, for example:

Sample Cover Letter

To the attention of *Name of Prospective Client*:

I am a freelance Spanish to English translator based in San Francisco, California, and I would like to offer my services to your agency. My specializations include legal and financial translations; due to my extensive experience in the banking industry, I have in-depth knowledge of financial terminology and industry procedures. My résumé is attached for your consideration.

After a successful ten-year career in banking, I launched my freelance translation business and am pursuing ATA certification in Spanish to English translation. Although I am a new translator, I am not a typical beginning translator. In addition to

my decade of work experience in the financial
industry, I have a B.A. in Spanish and recently
became a member of both the American Translators
Association and the Northern California Translators
Association. I also gained additional insights into
the translation industry by taking an online course
on translation business practices.

My home office computer equipment includes a desktop
and laptop computer with daily backups, high speed
Internet access and electronic fax. With each
freelance project I undertake, I guarantee high
quality work delivered on or before deadline and
prompt response to your phone calls and e-mails.
Please let me know if I can provide you with any
additional information.

In the cover letter above, the individual has little or no translation experience, but has work experience in an in-demand industry and probably good language skills. Again, if you have any translation experience, highlight it: "I recently launched my freelance translation business after gaining experience as a volunteer translator for Doctors Without Borders," etc. A cover letter like this could be easily pasted into an e-mail, or included in an appropriate field of an online application. For a paper letter, you would want to expand on the ideas in the letter above, for instance by providing specific examples of the financial industry terminology you know, or of your excellent work history at your previous job.

2.2 Finding your first clients

If you're starting out by applying to translation agencies, remember to play by their rules in order to maximize your chances of getting work. Most agencies have a translator application form on their websites; the "Contact Us" or "Opportunities" sections of agency websites are good places to look for these. Although it feels impersonal to apply for work this way, resist the urge to distinguish yourself by sending in a paper résumé if the agency requests an electronic one; what seems to you like a personal touch will only create more work for your potential client, and may get your application materials tossed without a second look. Along the same lines, most agencies prefer not to be contacted by phone unless you are applying for a specific position that they've advertised. If the online application form includes a "Comments" field, this is the place to ask for an in-person meeting or introduce yourself as a new translator in the area. For translation agencies in the United States, the website of the American Translators Association http://atanet.org is a good place to find the agency's web address, and the agency's profile on the ATA website may also indicate if it is currently accepting applications from new translators.

Whether applying to translation agencies or direct clients, there are a few basic rules to follow. You're applying for language work, so your application materials should be *error-free*. Make sure that everything you send out is proofed by yourself and at least one other person. When sending inquiries by e-mail, use a clear subject line, such as "German–English freelance inquiry." Don't disguise your intentions or make your message look like a response to an e-mail from the agency. State your language pairs prominently. As amazing as it may sound, many people neglect this simple step. Start your e-mail with a sentence such as, "I am a freelance English to Spanish translator and I would like to offer my services to your company."

Looking for work with direct clients has some positive and negative points for a beginning translator. As a newcomer to the profession, it can be helpful to have some of the safety nets that a translation agency offers; for example when you work for an agency, your work is almost always proofread before being sent to the end client, which guards against a true disaster if you make a mistake. However, direct clients, especially those located in areas where there are not many translators to choose from, may be more likely than a translation agency to take a chance on an inexperienced translator. Whereas a translation agency has a wide range of translators to choose from with no geographic restrictions, a direct client who wants to work with someone local has a bigger incentive to work with someone new.

If you'd like to work with direct clients, any large businesses, hospitals or school systems in your area are worth contacting, even if they don't have obvious international ties. Probably the best source of direct client contacts is international business organizations such as international chambers of commerce since you can be sure that the member companies use your non-English language in their business operations. Joining one of these organizations is also an excellent way to network with potential clients. Following is a list of the websites for some international chambers of commerce:

- New York chapter of the French-American Chamber of Commerce `http://faccnyc.org`

- New York chapter of the German-American Chamber of Commerce `http://gaccny.com`

- Chicago chapter of the Italian-American Chamber of Commerce `http://italianchamber.us`

- United States-Mexico Chamber of Commerce `http://usmcoc.org`

- Korean Chamber of Commerce and Industry in the U.S. `http://kocham.org`

- Japanese-American Chamber of Commerce, Silicon Valley `http://jaccsv.com`

- Polish-American Chamber of Commerce of Illinois `http://polishamericanbusiness.com`

- Swedish-American Chamber of Commerce `http://sacc-usa.org`

- Greek-American Chamber of Commerce `http://greekamericanchamber.org`

- Danish-American Chamber of Commerce in New York `http://daccny.com`

- Spain-US Chamber of Commerce `http://spainuscc.org`

- Vietnamese-American Chamber of Commerce, Minnesota `http://vietnamesechamber.com`

- Brazilian-American Chamber of Commerce of Florida `http://brazilchamber.org`

- Dutch-American Chamber of Commerce of Seattle `http://daccseattle.com`

- Asian Chamber of Commerce of Arizona `http://asianchamber.org`

Whatever route you'd like to take toward finding your first clients and building up your business, following are some tips that are applicable to almost every freelance translator's startup phase:

Be realistic. If you've never worked as a translator or interpreter before, starting out by contacting the United Nations or accepting a 90,000 word document on nuclear power plant safety procedures probably isn't the best way to start. Look for projects that you can do a great job on, and then use those projects to build up your business. Realize that depending on your languages and specializations, it could easily take a year to build up a base of regular clients.

Network, network, network. Although most translators are introverts by nature, many job search experts identify networking as the most powerful job search strategy, and starting your translation business is no exception. Talk about your business with everyone you know, and give them a business card; strike up a conversation with the receptionist in every office you wait in, and leave a business card. Volunteer for your local translators association and get to know the experienced translators in your language pair; prepare an "elevator speech" (a few sentences that summarize what you do) and be ready to give it to anyone who asks you about your job!

Think locally. Especially if you present yourself better in person than on paper, start out by asking for in-person meetings with every translation or interpreting agency in your local area. By asking for a meeting to learn more about the agency and talk about how you might fit in, you'll both benefit from the interaction. Don't be dissuaded if local agencies "have no work in your language combinations right now." By asking for an in-person meeting, you'll position yourself to step in when their needs change.

Blanket the field. One of the biggest mistakes made by beginning translators and interpreters is to assume that you'll be working full-time after sending out five or ten inquiries. On the contrary, you should expect no more than a one percent return rate on your cold-contacting efforts. A good start (emphasis: *start*) if you'd like to be working full-time would be to send out 300–500 résumés during your first year in business. Your prospective clients may include translation agencies in the U.S., agencies in countries where your other languages are spoken, and companies in your area that could use your services.

Join some associations. Membership in a professional association (see **Resources**, "Associations for translators and interpreters") establishes your seriousness as a linguist, and allows you to make contact with colleagues in your area. Even for established linguists, referrals from colleagues are an important source of work. If you're very resourceful and very lucky, you may even find a colleague in your language combination who is willing to take you on as an assistant or send some extra work your way.

Keep in touch. Instead of just firing off e-mails or making phone calls and then waiting to hear back from your potential clients, keep a log of the person you talked to or e-mailed with and what his or her response was to your inquiry. As you get more experience, periodically contact these people to let them know that you're still interested and available. Let them know what types of projects you've been working on, and let them know that you would be happy to help them out with similar jobs.

2.3 Building up your business

Once you've landed your first few clients, marketing yourself becomes easier in the sense that you have something to tell new prospective clients about, other than the fact that you're looking for work. In general, even a successful freelancer must spend at least ten percent of his or her time on marketing; for beginning translators this figure may increase to as much as 50 percent, and for those who have been in the business for many years, the need to market may fall by the wayside. However, many marketing experts caution that, "If you're not marketing, you're dying." While this advice may seem extreme, it's important for even experienced translators to prepare for the loss of a major client or a downturn in the economy by keeping up a steady flow of outbound promotion.

It's also important to distinguish between marketing for more work and marketing for better work. After a few years in business, many competent translators are busy most of the time, and do not need to market for more work. However, many of these people make the mistake of stopping their marketing efforts because they don't need more work. Here's where it's important to realize that marketing can lead to better work as well; work that pays a higher per-word or hourly rate, work that is more interesting, more flexible, or more ongoing, thereby lowering the translator's administrative costs. In reality, being busy all the time is a powerful lever to use with prospective new clients, since you can honestly tell them that in order to work for them, you will need to raise your rates. Following are some ways to keep the checks rolling in once you've gotten your business off the ground initially.

Please the clients you've got. While marketing to new clients is a worthy and even necessary endeavor, it's far easier to keep your existing clients coming back. If you're interested in building a sustainable business and a healthy income, regular clients who come to you, rather than the other way around, are key, since they allow you to spend your time working rather than looking for work. Doing a great job on every project, responding promptly to phone calls and e-mails, never missing a deadline, and being there for your clients in a pinch will help turn new clients into regulars.

Ask for referrals and testimonials. Preferably after you've just done an "above and beyond" job for a client, tactfully let him or her know that your business continues to grow thanks to referrals from satisfied clients. Better yet, ask your happy clients to put their experiences with you in writing to be posted on your website or included in future marketing materials.

Spread the word. As mentioned in the previous section, keep a log of all of the professional contacts you make, and periodically update these potential clients on your recent projects. The definition of "periodically" is up to you, but an appropriate frequency might be every one to three months; more often and your messages will grow annoying, less often and the agency representative may not remember you at all. It's possible to accomplish this task with a minimum of effort, by using a personalized e-mail such as this one:

```
Dear Name of Contact:

I am a freelance French to English translator
registered with your agency, and I'd like to update
you on some of my recent projects, in the event that
you have similar needs in the future.  In the past
few months, I translated and managed the editing for
```

```
a 90,000 word computer literacy manual, translated
two large documents of international airport
construction specifications and translated an auto
parts manufacturing quality manual.  In addition, I
recently completed a course entitled "French for
Lawyers," which covered the terminology of French
legal institutions.  I've attached my updated résumé
for your consideration, and I look forward to the
opportunity of working together in the future.
```

Keep cold-contacting. Many experienced translators estimate that of their new clients, approximately half come from cold contacts and half from word of mouth referrals. Whatever your level of experience, cold-contacting is important. If you're looking for agency clients, most agencies allow you to enter your information into their online database through the agency's website, and for direct clients you're probably best off contacting a project manager in the department you'd like to work for, for instance a localization project manager or international sales manager. If you're actively trying to build your business, set a goal of making 25 or more cold-contacts each week. Don't fall into the trap of expecting too many responses from too few contacts.

Keep networking. In a profession largely populated by independent contractors, networking gets you in touch with your colleagues and clients, either in person or electronically. Attending events for linguists is a great way to meet colleagues who may be in a position to refer work to you. If you're after new clients, consider joining a professional association in your target industry, whether this is signmaking, auto parts manufacturing, health care or law. Other networking endeavors worth considering are speaking to high school and college students considering careers in translation, teaching a class on getting started as a freelance translator or interpreter or taking on an intern from a local high school or college foreign language program.

Get creative. Sending your résumé to potential clients is important, but other marketing tactics can be as effective or more effective, especially with direct translation buyers. Put together a file of work you've done for previous clients (with their permission) and send it to prospective clients, offering to do the same for them. Present a compelling reason for potential clients to spend money on translation, i.e. "Are Spanish-speaking Internet users finding you, or your competition?" "Few Americans who visit France speak French, yet few French hotels and restaurants have websites in English," etc. For a potential "big fish" client, show your work—translate the prospect's brochure or website homepage, lay it out attractively, and ask for a meeting to discuss how you can help the client's business grow by making it more international. Starting an e-newsletter of interest to your clients and prospective clients is another useful marketing tool, since you're providing your clients with information they want while keeping your name fresh in their minds.

Become an expert. Writing, speaking and consulting about translation and interpreting are great ways to get your name recognized. Contact professional journals in your specializations and offer to write an article about translation issues in their industry; write a booklet on *Tips for Translation Buyers* and send it to potential direct clients; speak at professional conferences; post an article on *How to Speak Successfully When Using an Interpreter* on your website—by now you've got one, right?

2.4 Starting a part-time translation business

Depending on your financial and time resources, it may not be possible for you to make freelance translation or interpreting your full-time job right away. Starting a part-time business is a viable option, as long as you are careful to run your business in a professional way. Part-time freelance businesses can be split into two categories; taking on part-time translation or interpreting work in addition to another job, and taking on part-time translation or interpreting work as your only job.

If you already have another job and are interested in sideline work as a translator or interpreter, it's possible, and many successful freelancers start out this way, waiting until the translation or interpreting work can pay the bills before quitting another job. In this situation, you have the advantage of taking as long as you need to build your business up to the point where it replaces your current income. However, you also have the challenge of staying productive and available to both your full-time employer and your translation clients. Translation, like all international business, is often a fast-paced industry, and clients who contact you may need a response to their inquiry immediately, whether they're contacting you about working for them, or about doing revisions to a translation you've already completed. For this reason, if you'll be combining part-time translation work with a full-time job, it's important to choose your clients carefully so that you don't end up being unavailable when they need you. You may be better off taking lower-paying work that doesn't have a tight deadline, rather than higher-paying work that requires you to communicate with the translation client during your work day at your full-time job.

If you either don't want or don't need to work full-time, starting a part-time freelance business as your only job is a possibility as well. Depending on your geographical location and language pairs, your main challenge may be limiting your workload to your desired schedule. In theory, the on-call nature of most freelance translation and interpreting work lends itself well to part-time work, since it seems like you should be able to simply accept or turn down projects as your schedule allows. In practice, this isn't always the case. When a regular client calls, it's hard to say "No," since you want to help them out and keep them as a client; when no one calls, you can't do much about it. Still, many freelancers can and do make a go of it part-time. The main guideline to keep in mind is to organize and run your business just as professionally as you would if you were working full-time; your clients don't need to know that you work part-time unless they ask, so don't give them a reason to suspect that you're less committed than someone who works 40+ hours per week.

Part-timers of all flavors should pay special attention to business expenses as related to income. If you're interested in earning a healthy income even as a part-timer, keep in mind that all of your expenses are distributed over a smaller number of billable hours than they would be if you worked full-time. In this case, it's worth considering options that allow you to stay competitive and professional without spending top dollar; for instance trying a free or low-cost translation memory program, using a custom ring number instead of a dedicated business phone line, forgoing a laptop computer and cell phone unless you would use them for other reasons, and looking for second hand office furnishings.

2.5 Business skills you'll need

As a freelance translator or interpreter, you'll be exchanging the freedom of self-employment for the responsibility of finding your own work, charging a fair rate for this work, making sure you get paid, tracking your own tax liabilities, and many other tasks. In this section, we'll take a look at the non language-related skills that make for a successful freelance business.

Marketing. Unless you have a pre-existing client base, for instance a former employer who is interested in hiring you as a freelancer, you'll need to be able to market yourself. "Marketing" sounds like a scary and imposing concept at first, but if you've ever applied for a job, you've marketed yourself. Working as a freelancer is just a matter of applying for work over and over again until you build up a group of regular clients. One of the most important elements of marketing yourself as a translator or interpreter is to determine your comfort level with various sales techniques such as cold-contacting, networking, and public speaking.

Communicating. People do business with people they like, so while you don't want to grovel, it's important to hone your communications skills where your freelance business is concerned. First, you have to actually *do* the communicating; answer all business-related phone calls and e-mails as soon as possible, always within the same business day and preferably within an hour, and change your voice mail message or e-mail auto-responder when you'll be out of the office for more than one business day. Be honest about your availability and don't promise miracles that you can't deliver. Second, you need to communicate in a way that is positive and professional. Answer the phone cheerfully; when someone contacts you for work, thank them for thinking of you. When you call a client back and they've already found another linguist, thank them for contacting you and ask them to keep you in mind in the future, rather than getting angry that they didn't wait for your response.

Accounting. Like marketing, this is a concept that sounds frightening if you've never done it before. Especially if you've always worked as a salaried employee, working as a freelancer will require much more record-keeping than you've done before. However, at its most basic level, accounting for a freelancer consists of keeping records of your income and expenses, something that is definitely within your grasp. As with communicating, the most important aspect of accounting is to do it; record every payment as soon as you receive it and save receipts for every business expense in order to minimize your headaches at tax time.

Using technology. For translators, the days of pen and paper work are long gone, and you'll need to know how to use, at a minimum, the Internet, e-mail, and office software such as word processing and spreadsheet programs. Translation memory software can increase your productivity, and depending on your languages and specializations may be necessary to running a viable business, since some clients require it.

Billing and Collections. As a freelance translator or interpreter, you'll usually be responsible for billing your clients your-self and following up if they can't or won't pay. For most freelancers, a simple system of sending invoices by e-mail is enough, and you can keep track of your invoices either with a spreadsheet or on paper. Billing is the fun part, because your work is completed, and the expectation is that you'll be paid on time. When this doesn't happen, the situation is less sweet. You'll need to learn how to deal with clients who won't pay because of disagreements about issues such as the quality and timeliness of your work, and with clients who can't pay because of their own poor financial situations.

Dealing with highs and lows. While this is more of a psycho-logical skill than a business one, it's one of the most impor-tant assets that a freelancer needs. Whether you're trans-lating, interpreting or selling siding, the market goes up, and the market comes down. Unless you're either very lucky, a great planner, or both, you'll have weeks where you want to unplug your phone so that clients will stop calling, and weeks where you feel like you'll never be called by a client again. To make it as a freelancer, you'll need to deal with these peaks and valleys on several fronts. Most practically, you'll need to develop a budgeting strategy that keeps you from spending too much when your checking account is full and going into debt when work is lean. Men-tally, it's important to be productive even when you don't have much paying work, for instance by contacting new potential clients, updating your website, or catching up on your accounting.

2.6 Setting up your office and your business

While it's possible to spend many thousands of dollars setting up an office for your freelance translating or interpreting business, it's equally possible to get going with a minimal investment while maintaining a professional image.

Having a dedicated place to work is good for business on a

few fronts; it helps you stay focused and organized in your work environment, and at tax time it helps you claim office space as a business expense. At least at the outset, your office will probably be located in your home. Many translators and interpreters work from home for their entire careers, while some choose to rent office space once their businesses are on firm financial ground. Unless you have absolutely no space to set up an office in your home or have access to free office space outside your home, working from home is the most cost-effective option. As more libraries and places of business start to offer free or low-cost wireless Internet access, it's also an option to set up a very minimal office in your house, and do most of your work at another location on a laptop computer, although you may forgo the tax benefits of having a full-fledged home office.

In order to field inquiries from clients and research new client prospects, you'll need a phone with voice mail or an answering machine, and a computer with e-mail and Internet, preferably via a DSL, cable or satellite broadband connection that allows you to be on the phone and on line at the same time. Translators and interpreters at all levels will want to invest in a variety of general and specialized dictionaries, both print and electronic. You'll also need, at a minimum, office software on your computer. Translation memory (TM) software, also called CAT (computer-assisted translation) software is fast becoming a necessity as well, with prices ranging from free to several thousand dollars. A fax machine is convenient to have, but as e-mailed PDF files replace faxes, not a necessity if you live near a copy shop that offers incoming fax service; services such as Efax http://efax.com that deliver faxes to your e-mail inbox are also a good possibility. If you're looking to field client inquiries immediately and win a maximum number of assignments, a cell phone and/or wireless e-mail device will help keep you in contact, especially if you prefer the flexibility of working from a café or library when the walls of your home office start closing in!

Especially for translators, who often spend 40 and more hours a week at the computer, it's important to consider comfort and ergonomics when setting up your office. While you don't have to call in a consultant to correctly position your monitor, it's worth investing in a good-quality office chair, a computer desk that is correctly sized for you, and a monitor that is large enough that you're not constantly scrolling up and down pages all day. If cash is an issue, consider purchasing these items used. Put a bookshelf with your most commonly used reference materials within arm's reach as well.

2.7 Maximizing productivity

While one of the advantages of self-employment is flexibility, many translators and interpreters struggle to remain productive without the structure offered by a full-time job for an outside employer. All too often, what could be a successful freelance business founders when the translator or interpreter opts to clean closets, organize the basement or take an exercise class rather than working.

Following are some suggestions for staying on task when you're on your own time clock. If you already have above-average time management skills, you may be able to establish a productive routine without putting any of these measures into practice. If you're constantly overcome by the temptation to do anything but work, consider putting these systems into practice from day one!

- Strike a balance between enjoying the flexibility of freelancing and not letting it take over your work time. Too little flexibility will leave you wondering why you're freelancing in the first place, too much and you won't be earning any money. For example, block out certain times during which you allow yourself to do non-work activities such as exercising, grocery shopping, going to medical appointments, or getting together with friends. Limit non-work activities to these times only and consider yourself "at work" the rest of the time.

- Set quantifiable goals. Instead of amorphous targets such as "contact more new clients," draw up a list of concrete objectives that you must meet, such as "send out 20 résumés per week and follow up ten by phone."

- As much as possible, consider yourself "at work" when you're working from your home office. Close your office door. Don't answer your home phone unless you're expecting an important call, and let your family know that you are not to be interrupted except in an emergency.

- Limit the time you spend reading and responding to e-mail. This can be a huge time drain for freelancers, especially translators who are often contacted to provide quotes on translation projects. Unless you're expecting an important message, give yourself a set time to check e-mail, for example every hour on the hour for a maximum of ten minutes. A corollary to this is keeping separate personal and work e-mail accounts so that you are never tempted to spend work time on personal correspondence.

- Take a break by doing something useful. When you've had as much oil and gas terminology as you can stand, decompress for a few minutes by reading articles on a translators' website, writing a "tip of the day" for your website, or e-mailing a client to check in.

- If you're contacted frequently for the same information by prospective clients, make this available with as little effort as possible. Post your résumé on your website so that you can refer clients there. Keep a list of questions to ask new clients (rate, word count, subject matter, time of appointment, deadline, payment terms, etc.) within eyesight in your office so that you don't have to think about it when prospective clients call or e-mail you.

2.8 For working parents

Especially as compared with other types of freelance work, translation and interpreting are great career options for working parents. Although a freelance translation or interpreting career won't free you from the need to be available when clients call or to find reliable child care, it does allow flexibility, good income potential, and the freedom to expand or contract your working hours according to your other commitments.

Translation and interpreting offer several advantages for the working parent. In contrast to professions where freelancing is seen as the reward for years spent working as a full-time employee, most translators and interpreters start out as freelancers; the few in-house translation and interpreting jobs out there would rarely be offered to a beginner, so there's no stigma in starting out working for yourself. In addition, the project-based nature of most translation and interpreting assignments lends itself relatively well to part-time work on a flexible schedule.

For freelancers who have already built up a thriving business before having children, keeping the business going is primarily a matter of finding reliable child care, whether by paying a provider or by working when a partner or other family member can take over the family responsibilities, and of finding the energy to both work and take care of a small child.

If you're starting your business and your family at the same time, deciding if and when to schedule child care is a significant concern, as paying for child care when you're not earning money can quickly turn into a money-losing proposition. One translator who started her freelance business three months after her daughter was born comments:

> When I started out, I worked mostly at night and on weekends so I didn't have to pay a babysitter when I had no idea how much I would be making. After my first year, I hired a sitter four mornings a week after estimating conservatively on the financial side, and after two years my husband was able to quit his job

and work part-time, so now he takes over when I'm working.

As a working parent, one of the keys to a successful business is to capitalize on the advantages of your situation; rather than seeing your time constraints as a problem for clients, look for ways in which you can use them to advantage. As an interpreter, you might offer to work nights and weekends at weekday rates, minimizing your need for expensive child care and giving your employer an incentive to use you more. This could be especially valuable in settings such as hospitals, where interpreters are often needed outside of regular business hours. As a translator, you might offer to be available after hours, so that clients can get a jump on the next day's business by sending you a project to start as their work day ends, or you might look for clients in other time zones who will appreciate your unconventional schedule as an addition to their own work hours.

3 Home office setup, technology, and translation memory software

3.1 Preparing for your home office

While it's possible to spend many thousands of dollars setting up an office for your freelance translation business, it's equally possible to get going with a minimal investment while maintaining a professional image. Most translators work from home, so there's no stigma attached to doing so. At the same time, working from home poses its own set of challenges, including but not limited to: knowing how to manage your time so that your business is profitable; knowing when to take breaks and how to get enough exercise; resisting the temptation to work either too little or too much; setting rules for kids or other people in your household; staying on task and setting priorities.

3.2 The ups and downs of working from home

Especially if your current job involves a long commute, inconvenient hours or an unpleasant work environment, the thought of checking your e-mail in the morning while still wearing your pajamas and drinking a cup of coffee can seem like a slice of paradise. For many translators who work from home, the situation is an all around win, allowing them to be more in control of their schedules, work at times of the day when they have the most energy, and spend more time with family. At the same time, other freelance translators fail at self-employment primarily because they cannot work productively from home.

It's important to realize that there are jobs for translators that don't involve working from home as an independent contractor, for example you might find translation or project management work with a translation agency, technology company, hospital, school, etc. However in most cases you'll find the most work opportunities and highest pay by working for yourself. Many work-from-home consultants identify a few key personality traits that successful independent professionals share, for example: they are self-starters or "go-getters" who need very little external motivation; they understand their own positives and negatives; they are able to make good decisions quickly; they are energized by healthy competition rather than feeling intimidated by it, and they have a high level of self-discipline and will-power.

You'll want to assess where you stand on the issues presented by these questions, and also consider how well your current life situation lends itself to working independently from a home office. For example, do you have a location in your home that can be used as a home office? Keep in mind that in most (but not all) cases, in order to tax-deduct your home office expenses, your office must be a separate area that is used exclusively as an office, so if you set up your computer in a corner of the guest room, it's not an office. Does your family or living situation lend itself to working productively from home? Can you set guidelines for your spouse, room-mate, children, etc. on times that you are "at work" and not available except in the case of an emergency? If you have small children, can you afford to pay for child care while you work, even if you're not making a lot of money at the start? If you're planning on translation as your primary source of income, do you have six to nine months' income in savings to live off while the business gets going? It's important to consider these issues before you find yourself in a bad situation, and to see the relationship between planning and business success.

3.3 Necessary office equipment

Even if you need to purchase some pieces of computer or office equipment startup expenses for a freelance translation business should be relatively modest. If you already have an appropriate computer and a place to work from, your expenses might run only a few hundred dollars. Whether you have them already or not, here are a few items that make up the basic translation home office.

A computer is absolutely essential to a translator's work, and for backup purposes you may even want or need more than one computer. If you're prone to repetitive strain injury from typing, you may want to consider an ergonomic keyboard, although opinions differ on whether these work for everyone. If you live in an area where wireless Internet access is available in public places, a laptop with Wi-Fi capabilities can be a great way to escape the home office when you get lonely or claustrophobic.

A good sized computer monitor is also important, in order to minimize the amount of time you spend scrolling up and down. A 21-inch monitor is ideal, and some translators even install two video cards in their computer in order to accommodate two 21-inch monitors, one for the source document and one for the target, or one for the translation memory program and one for an online reference.

A comfortable desk and chair. You're going to be spending 90% or more of your time sitting at your desk, so make it comfortable and correctly sized for you; using your kitchen table or a card table isn't a great idea. Without a desk and chair that fit you, it can be tiring and uncomfortable to sit in the same position for hours at a time.

A phone. Whether or not you want or need a dedicated business phone line, it's crucial to be able to identify which calls are for your business so that you can answer the phone professionally. One option offered by most phone service providers is a *custom ring* number (sometimes called a *distinctive ring* number), which is an additional phone number that runs over the same physical line as your existing phone number. When a call comes to your business phone number, the phone will ring differently (normally two short rings instead of one long one), so that you know that the call is work related. A hands-free telephone headset can be really helpful when you need to type and talk at the same time, and you can purchase one inexpensively at an office supply store.

A way to receive faxes. Many hard copy documents are now scanned and e-mailed, so you may not receive faxes every day, but you do need some fax capability. A standalone fax machine is an obvious choice, or a fax modem connected to your computer, or a service such as Efax `http://efax.com` that converts faxes to e-mail. If you get very few faxes and live near a copy shop, the cheapest option of all is to receive your faxes at the shop and pay the per-page charge. If you have a fax machine or a fax modem, it should also be able to use a custom ring number, since most phone companies can assign at least two custom ring numbers to your existing phone line. If you want a fax machine, you might also consider a "multifunction machine" that acts as a fax machine, copier, printer and scanner.

A place to keep files. You'll need a filing box or cabinet to keep invoices, check stubs, tax information, hard copy translation documents, client information, etc.

Internet access is another essential element of the translation home office. For most translators, broadband Internet via cable, DSL or satellite is fast becoming a necessity. Especially if you use online dictionaries, you'll be connected to the Internet for most of the time you're working, which means that you can't make or receive phone calls if you have only dialup Internet access. In addition, many translation project files are very large and can take a long time to download over a dialup connection. In the event that your high-speed Internet access goes down, it's definitely helpful to have an Internet service provider that also allows dial-up access, giving you a backup method of Internet access when there's an outage.

A bookcase for dictionaries. Ideally, this should be within arm's reach of your desk so that you're not constantly getting up to get a book.

3.4 Organizing your business

When setting up your office, prepare for your business to grow. Following are some tips for organizing your translation business for maximum productivity.

Keep track of your assignments. When you only have one or two clients, it's relatively easy to remember what assignment is due when; add in five or ten others, and it's impossible. In order to avoid missing deadlines, make sure to log every project as it comes in, ideally in more than one place. For example, you might keep a spreadsheet using different color codes for each client, and record the project description, due date, and rate of pay. Then you could also keep a calendar next to your desk, with upcoming deadlines written in it. With this double-entry system, you're less likely to forget a deadline.

Keep track of your billings and collections. Without this simple step, you will soon have no business at all. Every time you issue an invoice, record the date, client's name, invoice number, amount of the invoice, and date due. Again, you can record this information either electronically, by using a spreadsheet or accounting software, or on paper. When a client pays you, note this wherever you recorded the invoice information, and also file the check stub or invoice marked "paid" in a folder for that client.

Know where your time goes. Especially if you're hoping to free-lance full-time, it's crucial to know how much you're working and how much you're actually making per hour. This can be as simple as writing on your calendar how many hours you worked and for which client, or can be done electronically too. This also helps you calculate your overhead expenses by showing how much time you're spending on non-billable work such as marketing and accounting.

Keep track of your business expenses. Depending on your tax and living situation, some or all of your business expenses such as office supplies, Internet access, auto mileage, phone bills, and even home office expenses like a portion of your mortgage payment and utilities may be tax deductible. However, you can get in serious tax trouble for deducting these expenses without having accurate records such as receipts and an auto mileage log.

Choose a reliable accounting system. There are a variety of ways to do your office bookkeeping, from a paper ledger book to a spreadsheet to a full-spectrum accounting software package. Whatever you choose, the key is to use your system consistently so that you don't end up wondering how much money you actually made or how much you spent on office expenses.

Keep only one calendar. One of the beautiful things about working from home is that you're not usually on a set schedule; one of the downsides of this is the tendency to double-book appointments or deadlines so that you end up scheduling a phone conference and a dentist appointment at the same time. Keep one calendar with personal and work appointments and deadlines to avoid conflicts.

Use a prioritized to-do list. One of the keys to remaining productive, especially in a home office setup, is to avoid interrupting your work to perform the many small administrative tasks that come up. When you remember something that you need to do, such as send out an invoice, respond to an e-mail, or update your website, don't perform the task right then unless absolutely necessary. Instead, record it, either on paper or electronically and prioritize it, for example as low/medium/high, or today/this week/when time allows. Then when you need a break from working, tackle the tasks in order of priority.

File! Instead of piling things on your desk to be lost, recycled, etc., force yourself to file anything that you're not using immediately. For example, keep a file for receipts to be entered into your business expense log, then transfer the receipts to a file for that year's business expenses once you've entered them.

3.5 Translation home office technology

Aside from translation memory software and possibly speech recognition software, the translation home office does not usually include out-of-the-ordinary technology. If you already work in a career where you use a computer, you probably know most of what it takes to run a translation home office. If your current job does not involve computer use, you may want to invest in a library or community college course in basic computer skills. Regardless of what your translation specializations are, every translator should know:

How to use advanced e-mail features. You should know what a *read receipt* is and how to request one or send one; how to *carbon copy* (CC) and *blind carbon copy* (BCC) someone on an e-mail and when to use both of these features; how to send and receive attachments; how to copy a text document and paste it into the body of an e-mail, and how to use *reply all* and *reply to sender* on e-mails that are sent to more than one person.

Sending and receiving attachments. You will receive and return most translation projects as e-mail attachments, so it's important to know how to attach a file to an e-mail and how to download an attachment when you receive one. It's also important to know where to find an attachment if your spam filter catches the message it's attached to. In addition, you should know how to use a program such as WinZip to zip groups of files into one attachment, and how to unzip these attachments when you receive them.

How to format documents. Often, clients will want their translated documents to look as much as possible like the source documents, so that the reader has the impression of looking at the same document in another language. To achieve this, it's important to know how to use different fonts, text boxes, tables, etc. in a word processor in order to properly format documents.

How to fill out and submit an online form. Especially if you will be applying to agencies, it's important to know how to use drop-down menus and text fields, how to paste your resumé into the appropriate field on an online form, and to remember to hit that Submit button only once! You should also know how to use browser features such as cookies, without which you won't be able to navigate certain websites.

How to use _Track Changes_ in a word processor. In the translation industry, the standard word processor is Microsoft Word, so if you use another word processor such as WordPerfect or OpenOffice.org, make sure that the program can save files in Microsoft Word format. For sending and receiving editing comments on your documents, you should know how to use Microsoft Word's _Track Changes_ feature to make corrections and insert comments.

How to effectively search on-line. Often during a translation assignment, you'll come across a term that isn't in any dictionary you use. The next step is to search for the term on-line and see what you find. You should know how to evaluate the trustworthiness of a website, how to use bilingual websites, and which search engines work best for you.

How to use web browser bookmarks. For sites you visit all the time, or visit once and want to remember, it's important to have a system of organized bookmarks stored in your web browser.

How to organize folders on your computer. Starting out with a folder called "Translation" isn't a bad idea, but once you have multiple clients with multiple projects, your files will quickly become impossible to find without a system of organized folders for each client and project.

How to rename a file. When you perform a translation, the client will often want you to translate the file name as well.

How to find a file. Once you've been translating for a few years or maybe even a few months, your hard drive will be filled with hundreds or thousands of files. Knowing how to effectively use the advanced features of *Find→File* or the equivalent on your computer is crucial.

How to back up your computer. This certainly isn't the most alluring aspect of home office computing, but it is arguably the most crucial. Since a translator is nearly 100% dependent on having a functional computer in order to work, think about what you would do if your computer simply wouldn't turn on one morning, if the hard drive died, or if the computer itself were destroyed by a flood or fire. A simple backup system might entail e-mailing yourself copies of projects in progress so that you can work on them from another computer. More advanced systems, which are an excellent idea, involve using some sort of removable device like a USB flash drive, Zip drive, CD-RW/DVD-RW, external hard drive or even another computer to back up your primary computer. Whatever backup system you choose, it is extremely helpful to have one that runs unattended, meaning that you don't have to remember to start it. You should also test your backups periodically so that you don't end up with a whole spindle of carefully marked backup CDs that turn out to be blank!

3.6 Translation technology and non-Western character sets

For translators who work from or into languages that use a Western character set, it is relatively easy to use software, view web pages, or create, edit and save documents in the non-English language. For translators working from or into languages that use non-Western character sets (i.e. Greek, Russian, Thai, Hebrew, Chinese, Japanese, Arabic and others), the situation can be more complex, and requires more planning of your computer system. There are three basic ways of implementing a non-Western character language on your computer.

First, you can use an operating system that is localized for the non-Western language; for example, Red Flag Linux, a Chinese Linux distribution, or the traditional or simplified Chinese version of Microsoft Windows or Mac OS X. If you use a localized operating system, all of the text that your computer displays will be in the non-Western language. This type of setup is a good option for translators who translate into a non-Western language, or who work in software localization, since it is helpful to see all of the messages generated by the computer in the non-Western language.

A second option is to use an English operating system with helper kits for your non-Western language. For example, Apple produces several non-Western language kits, which enable software such as word processors and web browsers to display and handle input of non-Western characters.

Finally, advances in Unicode technology have made it possible for many pieces of software to handle non-Western languages natively, meaning without the use of a helper program. Unicode is a standard that encodes the underlying characters in a language, rather than their visual representations, which enables almost all scripts and writing systems to be displayed on a computer through the use of *code points*, which are numbers that represent a language's characters. In this way, Unicode makes it possible to display languages with non-Western character sets, including right to left languages such as Arabic and Hebrew.

Before deciding what type of operating system you would like to use, it is important to think about what you will be using your computer for, other than standard tasks such as web browsing and word processing, which are now relatively accomodating of non-Western character sets. Especially if you translate between two languages with different character sets (for example French and Japanese), your needs may be very different from those of a translator who works between English and Spanish. It's also important to research the support offered for your language by the software that you would like to use. If the software has a relatively small market, is it fully localized, with the help files and documentation translated into your language, or is just the user interface localized? If you will be working in software localization, will clients want you to use an operating system in a language other than English? All of these are important items to consider when planning your computer system.

3.7 Speech recognition software

Depending on the type of translation you do and your stamina for typing, speech recognition software is somewhere between totally unnecessary and completely indispensable. For translators who don't mind doing a lot of typing, are relatively fast typists and don't have problems with repetitive strain injuries, speech recognition software is probably not necessary. If you have poor touch-typing skills, hate typing or have problems with your hands or arms hurting when you type a lot, speech recognition software can be a lifesaver.

Probably the most popular speech recognition software used by translators is ScanSoft's Dragon Naturally Speaking http://scansoft.com/naturallyspeaking, which starts at about $200. If you translate primarily from electronic format documents and use a translation memory program most of the time, speech recognition software may be of limited use. However, many legal and financial translators do a good deal of their work from hard copy or scanned documents and thus spend a lot of time typing directly into a word processing program. On projects like this, speech recognition software can help you work faster and with less strain to your hands and arms.

3.8 Translation memory software

Probably one of the most frequent topics of conversation among translators is whether to purchase translation memory software, which software works best for a particular application, how much the software costs, and on and on and on. Conceptually, translation memory software is not very complex. The most important thing to understand is the difference between *translation memory software* (TM; sometimes also referred to as *computer-assisted translation software,* or CAT) and *machine translation software* (MT). Translation memory software doesn't do the translation for you, rather it helps human translators work faster and more accurately by recycling material that has already been translated and suggesting a match between the old translation and the current one. Machine translation software is translation done entirely by a computer. Machine translation is currently the subject of a great deal of research and development, and it sometimes works well enough to get the basic idea of a document, but often produces comical or totally incomprehensible translations otherwise.

By definition, translation memory software only works with electronic documents; you can't take a piece of paper and run it through a translation memory program unless you retype it or scan it first using optical character recognition software (OCR), so if you translate mostly from hard copy or scanned documents, translation memory software is not very helpful. However, most translation memory programs can pull the text out of spreadsheets, HTML files, etc. Translation memory software works by *segmenting* your source document, meaning that the program breaks your document up into smaller chunks, normally sentences but sometimes paragraphs. Then, when a segment is ready to be translated, the program checks to see if you already translated a similar segment, and if it finds a match it suggests the match to you, theoretically resulting in a faster and more consistent translation. For example, if you already translated the sentence "This is a cat," and the next sentence was "This is a black cat," the TM program would suggest "This is a cat" as a match, so that you only had to type "black" in the target text box, instead of typing the whole sentence. Most TM programs display potential matches as percentages, for example the sentence "This is a dog" would be a 75% match with the sentence "This is a cat," since only one of the four words is different. This matching feature can be particularly helpful when your translation client has specific terms that they want you to use throughout the document, for example to always use "President and Chief Executive Officer" for the chairman of the company. Most translation memory packages use the file terms *uncleaned* and *cleaned*; an uncleaned file contains the source text and the electronic codes used by the translation memory program, while the cleaned file contains only the target text.

Another use of translation memory tools, although a task that some TM tools don't do very well, is *alignment*. Alignment means taking the source and target versions of a document, and matching them up so that you have pairs of sentences, one in the source language and one in the target language. This way, you can create a bilingual glossary out of your old translated documents. In practice, this function can be annoying to use; if the source and target sentence pairs don't match up exactly, it requires a lot of time on the translator's part to manually fix the mis-aligned segments.

Translation memory software is also somewhat controversial among translators. One of the reasons for this is that translation clients who are aware of TM software's capabilities will often ask for discounts on repetitive documents; for example the client will use the software to analyze a document, and tell you that although the document is 2,782 words, they only want to pay for 2,582, because there are 200 words that are repeated in the document. Or, a client might ask you to reuse the translation memory file from an old translation, and want to pay only for the new words translated; for example if the client is putting out a new version of a software manual, they might want to pay you to translate only the updated parts. Some translators are completely opposed to giving discounts for the use of TM software, on the grounds that they pay to acquire and maintain the software, they do the work on the translation, and even if a segment is a 100% match with a previously translated one, the translator still has to read the segment and sometimes make other adjustments as well. On the other hand, translation agencies and even some direct clients are very familiar with the potential cost savings of translation memory software, and they in turn want to reap some of the benefits too. Many translators rightly point out that when there are cost savings from using TM, three players in the situation want to benefit: the translator, the translation agency, and the end client, and obviously someone has to forgo his or her percentage of the savings.

One issue with translation memory software is that there are a variety of programs available at different price levels and with different features, and these programs are not always compatible with each other. The TMX (Translation Memory eXchange) and XLIFF (XML Localization Interchange File Format) standards are changing this situation somewhat, and some newcomers to the market, such as Heartsome, use these open standards, and guarantee that translation memories generated by their software can be re-used with market leaders such as Trados, SDLX, and Déjà Vu.

3.8.1 Trados

Trados `http://translationzone.com` is the market leader translation memory tool, and probably the tool most requested by translation agencies. It works from within Microsoft Word, so you must also have a current version of MS Word to use Trados. Trados is, by most freelancers' standards, expensive: $895 for the freelance edition of Version 7, although group buying discounts are sometimes available through translation websites. Trados, like many translation memory programs, is not always easy to learn to use, and can require additional training outside the resources that come with it. Two terms that you'll need to know when working with Trados: *uncleaned* files are the files generated by MS Word that have the Trados segment markers still in them, and *cleaned* files are the files that have the markers removed.

3.8.2 SDLX

SDLX http://sdlx.com is produced by SDL, which acquired Trados in 2005. As of this writing, the standard edition of SDLX is $695. You can also download a fully functional 30-day trial copy of SDLX for free. SDLX has the reputation of being somewhat more stable and easier to use than Trados, but this depends on the user's level of computer skills. **Note**: Due to SDL, Inc's (the makers of SDLX) purchase of Trados in the summer of 2005, these two tools have been merged into SDL Trados 2006. For more information, see TranslationZone http://www.translationzone.com.

3.8.3 Déjà Vu

Déjà Vu http://atril.com is very popular with European translators and is becoming more so in the United States. Unlike Trados, Déjà Vu (sometimes referred to as DVX since it is now in version 10) is a standalone application that runs by itself, rather than from within Microsoft Word. The standard edition of DVX costs $603.

3.8.4 Wordfast

Wordfast http://wordfast.net is a TM application that is quite similar to Trados in look and feel; it also works from within Microsoft Word. Wordfast costs €180 for a license that is good for three years of upgrades.

3.8.5 Heartsome

Heartsome http://heartsome.net, developed in Singapore, is a relative newcomer to the TM industry, but has gained a lot of attention lately. Heartsome uses the XLIFF standard and is currently the only commercial TM application that will run on a Linux computer system and support the OpenOffice.org free office suite's file formats. Heartsome is also quite affordable; the translation editor is $88 and the full translation suite is $398.

3.8.6 OmegaT

OmegaT `http://omegat.org` is the best-known free TM application. It is developed by a team of volunteers and has a very active user community. Like DVX, it is a standalone application that does not require Microsoft Word. And it really is free! OmegaT runs on Windows, MacOS X and Linux, and will also work with files from the free OpenOffice.org office suite.

3.8.7 WordFisher

WordFisher `http://wordfisher.com` is another free translation tool, written by a Hungarian translator, that has a lot of features for the price! WordFisher is a small-scale application for translators who find that the higher-priced translation memory applications are overpowered for what they need to do. For translators who don't need the functionality of a high-end TM tool, Wordfisher is very easy to learn to use and has some excellent features. It requires a current version of Microsoft Word.

3.8.8 across

across `http://across.net`, produced in Germany, is another tool that integrates a translation editor, translation memory engine, terminology system and some project management tools. Like many other programs, across offers several editions; the Personal Edition for freelancers costs €399. across is a standalone application running on its own, rather than from within another program such as Microsoft Word.

3.9 Choosing a computer system

Probably the most popular computer setup for freelance translators is a desktop computer with a Windows operating system and Microsoft Office. However, translators do also successfully use Mac OS X or Linux systems as well. While some translation clients will want their translators to run a certain operating system, most clients don't have strong preferences as long as the completed translation files are delivered in the correct format. Before selecting a computer system, it is important to decide what additional software you would like to use. For example, while most of the market leader translation memory applications such as SDL, Trados and Wordfast do not officially support OS X, their applications will often run on it with some fine-tuning, without using any additional software. Applications such as Heartsome and OmegaT are relatively platform-independent, and will run on Windows, Mac or Linux systems. In addition, CrossOver Office http://www.codeweavers.com enables Linux users to run a wide variety of Windows applications (such as Microsoft Office) on Linux without a Windows license. For example, the Wordfast translation memory application, which runs from within Microsoft Word, will run on Linux using CrossOver office.

4 Rates, contracts and terms of service

4.1 Setting your translation rates

Possibly the most anxiety-provoking aspect of launching your translation business is deciding how much to charge. Charge too much and you'll be priced out of the market; charge too little and you'll be working overtime just to make ends meet. The easiest way to remove some of the anxiety from this decision is to gather some objective data such as how much money you would like to make, and how much it will cost you to run your business.

Every language combination and specialization has a range of rates; for example, translators of Asian languages into English will almost invariably earn more than translators of European languages into English, although there are individual translators who will always be the exception to this rule. In addition, how much you need to charge depends on your cost of living. An English to Spanish translator living in rural Mexico can afford to work for lower rates than his or her colleague who lives in Manhattan. Some translators get very angry about these global outsourcing possibilities, but the reality is that they are just a function of the variation in global costs of living; in a developing country, someone earning $15.00 an hour can live quite well, while someone making $75.00 an hour in Geneva may be barely getting by.

Adding to the pricing confusion is that most people are used to calculating their wages by the hour, while most translation projects are paid by the word. Depending on the language combination involved, individual translators will want to be paid either by the source or the target word. For example, Romance languages such as French and Spanish take about 30% more words than English to communicate the same text. So, translators of French or Spanish into English will usually ask to be paid by the source word, whereas translators working in the opposite direction will earn more money by being paid by the target word. If there is an industry standard, it is often to set payment based on the source word count, since this lets the client and the translator know how much the project will cost before it has even begun. For character-based languages such as Japanese and Chinese, the word count is most often based on the number of English words regardless of the direction of the translation.

Beginning translators often don't know how to estimate how long a translation will take; so they don't know how to set their per-word rates in order to reach their target hourly rate of pay. Whereas an experienced linguist knows approximately how many words per hour he or she translates when working on various types of documents (general, technical, highly technical, hand-written, hard copy, HTML, etc.), there is no way to know this if you haven't done much translation; you simply have to time yourself while you translate to see how fast you work. In general, a translator who is a relatively fast typist (or uses speech recognition software that works well) can translate 400–600 words per hour or 2,000–3,000 words per day, but this is only a ballpark figure. When working on a highly technical document with few repetitions, or on a handwritten document that is difficult to read, even an experienced translator might produce just a few hundred words per hour.

Non-billable time is another variable in the pricing equation. When you have a full-time job for an employer, you are normally paid to work 40 hours a week, whether or not all of those hours are spent working productively. As a self-employed freelancer, you will be paid only when you are actually translating. Tasks like marketing, billing, collections, e-mailing back and forth with current and prospective clients, providing rate quotes for upcoming projects, and downtime when you have no work, are all off the clock—work time that you have to put in but that you don't get paid for. When all of these tasks are added up, most freelancers will spend at least 25% of their time on non-billable work, and it's not unreasonable to estimate up to 50% non-billable time when you add in work slowdown times when you would like to be working, but aren't.

Completing the following two charts will help you determine how to set your rates for translation. In the *Sample* column are example figures to use for comparison. Fill in your own figures in the right-hand column.

Table 4.1: BILLABLE HOURS

	Sample	Your estimate
Hours per week you would like to work	40	
Weeks per year you would like to work (subtract vacation weeks)	48	
Total working hours per year (hours per week x weeks per year)	**1,920**	
Sick hours per month x 12 months	96	
Legal holiday hours (7 days per year)	56	
New total working hours per year (previous total, minus sick and holiday hours)	**1,768**	
Non-billable time (25–50% of total: marketing, accounting, etc)	700	
Billable hours per year	**1,068**	

Table 4.2: HOURLY RATES

	Sample	Your estimate
Your salary goal	$40,000	
Taxes (15–50% of salary)	$6,000	
Internet, website hosting, phone, fax, cell phone (sample= $100/mo x 12 mos)	$1,200	
Memberships and professional development (including association dues, conferences, etc.)	$1,500	
Marketing and advertising (could be much more or less)	$500	
Office rent (no total given since most translators work from home; if you plan to rent office space, write it here)	$0	
Office supplies (envelopes, printer paper, pens, etc)	$500	
Computer hardware and software (depends heavily on what you need to purchase)	$800	
Auto and travel expenses (could be $0 if you never travel for work, or several thousand dollars if you attend multiple conferences or travel to visit clients)	$250	
Total cost of business operation	**$50,750**	
Profit goal (to be reinvested in business; sample is 10%)	$5,000	
Total revenue required	**$55,750**	
Required hourly rate (Total revenue divided by billable hours from chart above; sample is $55,750/1068)	**$52.20**	

Once you have this hourly rate worksheet completed, you've completed a major step in pricing your translation services. Your next step is to determine how you're going to arrive at that hourly rate. For example if you want to earn $60.00 an hour, you can achieve this by translating 600 words per hour at 10 cents per word, 400 words per hour at 15 cents per word or 300 words per hour at 20 cents per word. In order to do this, you need to know how fast you work (the only way to figure this out is to time yourself while you do some translations) and what the range of rates for your language pair(s) and specialization(s) is.

For example, you might look at rate surveys on Translators Cafe `http://translatorscafe.com` or ProZ.com `http://proz.com`, or look at websites of translators in your language pair to see if they publish their rates. Some translators, although not all, are also willing to discuss rates with their colleagues.

4.2 Rate sheets

Whether or not you publish or discuss your rates, it's important to have a rate sheet somewhere, even if it's just for your own use. Your base rate will cover most jobs, but clients will also ask about other types of services, so you should have the following in mind:

Standard rates. These are the rates that you apply to most translation projects that come across your desk. Generally, this would include projects that are in one of your usual areas of specialization, are in a format that you normally handle, and don't involve working overtime to meet the deadline.

Volume discount. Many translators offer a lower per-word rate for larger projects, since a large project allows you to spend your time working instead of looking for work, and decreases your administrative overhead for things like billing and collections. The flip side of this (and why not all translators offer a volume discount) is that in the worst case scenario, a large project can actually cause you problems if you have to turn down work from other regular clients who contact you while you're tied up with the big project. Large projects are also problematic if the client pays late or doesn't pay.

Rush charge. Nearly every translation project is a rush in some sense, but not infrequently something is a real rush. For example a client might ask you to receive a document at 4PM and return it by 9AM, or to work on a weekend, or to translate a 4,000 word document in 24 hours. Normally these jobs are charged at a higher rate than your base rate, although for a regular client some translators waive their usual rush charges.

Minimum charge. Even if a translation involves only a few words (and these projects come up; for example when a company wants their marketing slogan translated into fourteen languages), you still have to communicate with the client, issue an invoice, deposit the check, follow up if the client doesn't pay, etc. For this reason, most translators have a minimum charge of somewhere between $20 and $50 for projects that are under a certain word count, such as $25 for 200 words or fewer.

Editing rate. Most reputable translation agencies will have every translation proofed by another translator, so you may be interested in offering this service. Editing rates are normally one-quarter to one-third of your usual translation rate.

Translation memory discounts. Some of your clients will want to make more money for themselves or their clients by asking for a discount when you use translation memory software on a document that is very repetitive. Whether you do this or not is up to you. Some translators offer no discount at all, others only for 100% matches, still others offer a stepped pricing plan for *fuzzy matches*, for example charging 60% of their regular rate for 75–99% matches, 80% of their regular rate for 50–74% matches, etc. If you choose to offer this type of discount, most translation memory packages have tools to report the match percentages in your document.

4.3 Contracts or work for hire agreements

Many clients will ask their freelance translators to sign contracts or *work for hire* agreements before beginning work. While these are often quite harmless in nature and not something to be concerned about, it's important to read what you're signing and to make sure that you're not agreeing to a clause that you will later regret. These contract clauses are mostly applicable if you work through translation agencies. For example, you should carefully consider, possibly with the advice of a lawyer, whether you will agree to terms such as:

- Agreeing not to get paid until the end client pays the agency. Of all the terms that translators are asked to accept, this is probably the most difficult. In one sense, it's understandable that an agency doesn't want to take the risk of having to pay tens of thousands of dollars to translators for a project that the agency itself is never paid for. In addition, if a translator returns poor quality work, the agency doesn't want to be responsible in the event that the end client refuses to pay. On the other hand, the agency's role as a middleman between the translator and the end client involves some financial risks, such as non-payment on the part of the end client. If you agree to this type of clause, it is important to realize that you are accepting some risk of non-payment yourself.

- Agreeing to indemnify (hold harmless) the client against lawsuits and/or claims resulting from your translation. If you sign a contract with this type of clause, make sure that you carry your own professional liability or *errors and omissions* (E&O) insurance in case one of your clients is sued because of an error in your translation. The client should have a quality control system in place so that an error by one translator doesn't have a disastrous effect on the final project, but not every client will have this. This type of contract clause is more of a concern if you work for direct clients, who may be less likely to have your work edited or proofread before distributing it.

- Agreeing not to accept or solicit work from the agency's clients. Most intermediaries between end clients and free-lancers, not just translation agencies, require this type of *non-compete* agreement. It's perfectly reasonable to ask that you not go behind the agency's back and ask the end client to hire you to translate for them directly. However unless you and the agency compare your client lists (something the agency will probably be unwilling to do) you can't really know that you're not working for one of them.

- Agreeing not to subcontract work to another translator. This is another fairly common and reasonable clause, just make sure you read it before signing, and if you commit to doing all the work yourself, don't share it with someone else.

- Agreeing to abide by confidentiality standards. Especially if you work in legal, financial or patent translation, you will probably come into contact with trade secrets, confidential financial information, patent applications, etc. If you sign this type of document, again it is important to read and abide by its provisions. For example, financial translators might be required to agree not to engage in insider trading as a result of their knowledge of a company's financial information before it is released to the public. This type of document is often referred to as a non-disclosure agreement or NDA.

- Agreeing to submit to a credit check, criminal background check or financial review in order to be *bonded*. Like the confidentiality agreement described above, there are good reasons why some translators have to be bonded (insured against stealing because of information that they have access to). For example if you work with a bank's clients' financial information, or translate information about a mutual fund's identity verification procedures, you have access to information that would allow you to steal money from the company or its clients. In order to be bonded, most insurance or bonding companies will investigate your financial records and/or criminal background. Just make sure you are clear on what you're agreeing to when you sign this clause, and that you understand what information about you the company is going to collect or ask for. If you have a past criminal background, make sure you understand what types of charges, arrests or convictions must be reported.

If you find a clause in a contract that you don't want to sign, you have a few options. You could cross out the clause in question, modify it, or refuse to sign the contract completely. Whether or not this is successful depends on the client. Some agencies will agree to a change, others will refuse to work with you if you don't sign their contract. The most important thing is to realize that if you sign a contract, its terms are legally enforceable, even if an agency employee tells you, "I can't imagine we would ever really enforce that..." If the client wouldn't enforce the clause, it shouldn't be in their contract. Remember that although it is intimidating to be presented with a contract as a prerequisite for a certain job, you are an equal party to the contract and are entitled to object to terms that are unfair to you. Also, although contracts don't appear to be negotiable most of the time, they often are negotiable, and in any event you are highly unlikely to lose a client simply because you have questioned one of their contract's clauses.

4.4 Terms of service

Just as a client may ask you to sign a contract, so you as a translator may ask your own existing or potential clients to agree to your terms of service. Before accepting any work, it is important to agree on terms of service with the client; some clients will tell you what their usual terms of service are, but there is often some room for negotiation as well. Depending on who the client is, you might ask them to sign a printed copy of your terms of service, or you might send an e-mail summarizing what your terms of service are. *Your agreement with the client should first summarize the project, per-word rate, whether the word count is based on the source or target count, the project deadline, the file format, and the delivery method.* Even with a client that you work for regularly, you should always summarize the basic elements of the project so that everyone is in agreement before you start work. With a regular client, this would probably take the form of an e-mail confirming the project's due date and payment rate, along with any special instructions.

Although you should decide your own terms of service, following is a sample letter that a translator might send to a client to confirm the details of a project before beginning work.

Sample terms of service letter

Dear *Name of Person assigning you the project:*

Thank you very much for contacting me about your upcoming translation project. So that we are in agreement about the specifications for this project before I begin work, I am sending you a summary of the project as I understand it, along with my basic terms of service. Please either reply to this e-mail indicating your agreement with these specifications and terms, or let me know if there is anything to be changed.

Description of project: Translate ABC, Inc. annual report from English to German

Approximate word count: 26,000 words

Rate: X cents per source word *(always specify if the word count is based on the source or target word count)*

Deadline: 9AM EST on May 1, 2007, as long as project source files are sent to the translator by the close of business on April 5, 2007

File format: Source files in PDF, translation to be delivered in Microsoft Word, respecting the format of the source document as much as possible

Special instructions: *(request that the client provide you with any special instructions about the project)*

Terms of service: Payment will be made in full by check in U.S. dollars drawn on a U.S. bank, within 30 days of delivery of the translation. Late payments may be subject to a late fee of X dollars per day.

Following this summary of the project specifications, you should include your own terms of service, in addition to payment terms as shown above. Following are some of the more common terms of service used by freelance translators. Not all of these terms will apply to every translator, so it is important to chose the ones that are important for you, and to modify them to your particular situation.

- *No claims will be considered after X days from the date of invoice.* You need to set a time frame within which the agency can ask you for revisions, tell you that there's a problem with the translation, etc. You don't want an agency coming back several months later to complain about a project that you barely remember working on, but you do need to give the agency time to solicit feedback from their end client. So, a time limit of somewhere between two weeks and one month is probably reasonable.

- *Within the limits of the law, all claims will be limited to the amount of this invoice.* A clause such as this lets the client know that if they're not satisfied with your work, the most they can do is refuse to pay you; they can't, for example, ask you to forgo your own payment *and* reimburse them for the cost of additional editing of your translation. However, especially if you translate for direct clients, there may be situations where the client is legally allowed to sue you for damages if they are sued as a result of errors in your translation. Make sure you are clear on this before accepting work from a client that is not a translation agency. Translators who work for direct clients should strongly consider carrying professional liability/Errors and Omissions insurance, in the event that a client pursues a legal or financial claim against you for errors in your work. The American Translators Association offers this type of insurance through an affiliated insurance agency, and independent agents may sell it as well.

- *The client's terms of service are not in effect until approved in writing by the translator.* This prevents the client from holding you responsible for abiding by a contract that you haven't signed. For example, the client cannot come back to you after the project and say, "Our translator contract specifies that you don't get paid until the client pays us."

- *If the client is employed by an end client or third party, the translator's business agreement is with the client only. The client must pay the translator as agreed upon, regardless of the end client or third party's payment policies.* In essence, you are letting your client (a translation agency or freelance project manager) know that if the end client doesn't pay them, the client still has to pay you. The end client is not *your* client.

- *The translator retains copyright to the translation until the invoice for the translation has been paid in full.* When you contract with a client to do a translation for hire, you give up your copyright to the translated work, unless the contract specifies otherwise. However, if the client never pays you or doesn't pay in full, they haven't upheld their end of the work for hire agreement. Basically, this clause gives you the option of pursuing the client or end client for copyright violations if they use your translation without paying you.

- *If the translation project is canceled after a project assignment has been made, the translator will be paid for all work completed up to the time of cancellation.* Sometimes a client will send you the wrong file, cancel a project or scale a project down in size after you have already started working. While you shouldn't expect to be paid for the entire project unless you've completed it, you should be paid for the part of the work that you've already done, since you obviously can't do anything else with the translation. With a reputable client this shouldn't be a problem as long as the reason for the cancellation is clearly the client's mistake.

- *If the client is not satisfied with the translator's work, the translator must be given an opportunity to correct the translation before payment terms or rates are changed.* No matter how skilled

you are as a translator, some clients will not be fully satisfied with your work. Including this type of clause will
(hopefully!) protect you against clients who say that they're
not happy with your work, and will not pay you, or take a
discount on the agreed-upon price. Before the client brings
up any change in the agreed-upon payment terms, they
should let you know specifically what is wrong with the
translation, and give you the chance to correct it.

4.5 Researching your potential clients

As we'll discuss later in this chapter, some problems with clients
are unavoidable; no matter how well you set things up in advance
and how well you know your clients, issues come up and you'll
need to resolve them. In the case of payment and contract issues,
the best defense is definitely a good offense; it's infinitely easier
to lay the groundwork correctly for a project than to chase after a
client for months for your money, or lose a valuable client because
of a misunderstanding.

The most important first step in making sure you get paid is
to know who your client is. Dealing with someone who gives
you only an e-mail address or cell phone number as contact information is a setup for non-payment, since you will have no
recourse if the cell phone number or e-mail address in question
is discontinued when you need to get paid. At the very least,
you should get every client's full name or business name, website
address, mailing address (if the address is a P.O. box, ask for a
physical address as well), and phone and fax numbers. If you're
suspicious about the client's legitimacy, this information should
let you do at least a brief search; for example you could Google
the client, call directory assistance and see if the phone number
you get matches the phone number the client gave you, etc. If the
client has a website, you can also find out the information that the
client provided when they registered their website domain name.
The easiest way to do this is via a website such as Whois.Net
http://whois.net, where you can enter the client's domain

name and immediately find out who the technical and billing contacts for the domain are. For this reason (ability to trace a client through a third party), it is also wise to beware of clients who will only provide you with a free e-mail address, for example Hotmail, Yahoo, Gmail, etc. Although webmail is very useful for some purposes, one of the unfortunate attractions of free e-mail accounts is that you don't have to provide any verifiable information about yourself to get one. Therefore it is very easy for someone to use a free e-mail address and then cancel it and simply disappear, which is impossible if your e-mail account is through a paid Internet service provider who has your contact and billing information. For clients who are established businesses or large translation agencies, you may also have the option of doing a credit check on the client through one of the large credit bureaus such as Experian http://experian.com.

Another truly excellent way to investigate potential clients is via a translation industry payment practices list. Probably the most widely-used list is Ted Wozniak's Yahoo Payment Practices http://trwenterprises.com/payment_practices.htm. On this list, and others like it such as the ProZ Blue Board http://proz.com/bb (available only to paying members), you can post a query about a potential translation client, and other translators will respond to you and tell you their experiences working with this client. Based on the information given, the client will receive a score; on Ted Wozniak's list the score is on a one to five scale with five being the best rating. This is mostly applicable if you work with translation agencies, but sometimes you will get responses about direct clients as well.

It is also acceptable and even advisable to ask a potential client for references from other translators who work for them. You might be uncomfortable or feel impolite doing this the first few times, but it's important to remember that if you work for a client who promises to pay you when the project is done, you are *extending credit* to the client by working without an up-front payment. Since you cannot resell the translation somewhere else if the client doesn't pay you, you are effectively loaning the client your time for the promise of future payment. Don't do this lightly;

set the situation up so that you have the best possible chance of getting paid.

4.6 Standard payment terms and methods

In the United States, the most common payment terms when freelance translators work for translation agencies are that the agency will pay you within 30 days of the date of your invoice, referred to in the industry as *Net 30*. These payment terms are good for translators (or at least better than Net 60 or 90!) because your cash flow is only a month behind your work flow; if you send in an invoice on March 30, you get paid by April 30, at least in theory. In practice, many agencies will pay a little later than Net 30, or may ask you to invoice them once a month for all of your work, and they will pay you 30 days after that, referred to as *30 Days End of Month* or *Net 30 EOM*. Most U.S. agencies will pay by check in U.S. dollars, so you just deposit the check at your bank. Some will pay by PayPal, and this is a good way to ask clients who aren't established agencies to pay since you receive the money right away. Some U.S. agencies are starting to pay by ACH transfer, for which most banks will not charge a fee.

In other parts of the world, payment terms vary widely. Payment terms in Europe are almost invariably longer than Net 30. Many European clients will want to pay you Net 60, 60 Days EOM, or even Net 90, and may not be willing to pay sooner. As long as you get paid eventually, the only issue with these payment terms is that you wait a long time for your money, and if there is a problem with the payment you may wait even longer. For example if you work on a translation project from March 2–5 with terms of 60 Days EOM, you send the invoice March 31 and the payment is scheduled for June 30, by which time it is almost three months since you started the translation. If you live in the U.S., most agencies in Europe will pay by wire transfer, so it is important to find out what kinds of fees your bank charges for wire transfers. Normally an agency will ask for your bank's *routing number* (also called *ABA code*), *Swift code* (call your bank to get this) and your account number in order to complete a wire transfer.

Currency exchange fluctuations are another issue to consider if you work for clients outside the U.S. For example, as discussed above, many agencies in Europe will pay up to three months after the project is completed, which can leave quite a bit of room for exchange rate fluctuation before the job is paid. If you're dealing with clients in a country where the currency could potentially fall against the dollar, or with a very large project where even a small fluctuation could make a big difference in your pay, it's important to plan ahead. For example, you might agree on a rate in dollars, which effectively asks the client to absorb the risk or benefit of a currency fluctuation. Or, you might keep a separate foreign bank account in a country where you do a lot of business; if you do this, make sure to check with an accountant as to your tax responsibilities for accounts held outside the U.S.

Some clients will tell you up front that due to either the size of the project or their own cash flow situation, they cannot pay you until the end client pays them. If you agree to work for this client anyway, you are going into the situation knowing that there is a chance that you will not be paid on time or maybe at all. If you loan a friend money until his or her next paycheck, you know that you may not be repaid—the friend could lose the job, the paycheck could bounce, or other expenses could be more important than paying you back. Likewise, if you agree to get paid when your client (usually a translation agency) gets paid, you are knowingly taking a risk, so resist the urge to blame the client if you don't get paid!

4.7 Setting the stage for payment

Maximize your chances of getting paid on time by billing your client in a timely manner and using a well-organized invoicing system. Following is an example of what a translation invoice looks like; if your freelance business is incorporated, you will have an *Employer Identification Number* (EIN); if you are a sole proprietor, you would include your Social Security number (SSN) here, which the client needs in order to send you a 1099 form if you earn more than $600 from them in a year.

Sample Invoice

Invoice

Name of Translator d/b/a

Your Business Name

Street Address

City, State, Zip Code

Phone number

Email address

EIN: *XX-XXXXX*/SSN: *XXX-XX-XXXX*

Please make checks payable to: *Your Name or Your Business Name*

Invoice Number: *Include an invoice number that has some logic to it; for example the year and then a reference number (200501, etc) or your initials and then a number (JGF01, etc).*

Billed to: *Name of Client*

Client Contact: *Name of the Person who assigned the project to you*

Date: *Date you are issuing the invoice*

Payment due: *Make sure you and the client agree on the payment terms*

Agency Project Number: *Many clients will give you their own job number to include here.*

Description of Project: *Include a short description of the project, such as "Translate market research surveys from English to Spanish"*

Word Count: *Include the number of words, and make sure you and the client agree on whether you are charging by the source or target word count*

Rate: *Include the per-word or per-hour rate here*

Total Amount: *Include the total amount the client owes you.*

The easiest way to send your invoices, unless the client has an-other system, is to send them with the translation when you submit it. This way, if the client received your translation, you know that they received your invoice too. Some clients may want you to invoice them at the end of the month, or to submit your invoice to a special e-mail address just for invoices. If this is the case, just make sure that the client confirms that they received your invoice. Some agencies outside the U.S. may have other invoice requirements, for example that your invoice has to be signed by hand and sent by postal mail. Normally, the client is not expected to pay your banking fees (such as a fee that your bank charges when you receive a wire transfer), so don't add these to the invoice unless you have cleared it in advance with the client. Likewise, the client should not charge you for their bank fees (such as the fee that they have to pay to wire money) unless they have cleared it with you in advance.

4.8 When things don't go as planned...

If you haven't received the client's payment within the specified time frame, wait an appropriate amount of time and then politely remind the client that the payment is due. An "appropriate" amount of time is up to you; if the payment terms are Net 30, most translators would wait one to two weeks before contacting the client. Nine times out of ten, the problem will be resolved immediately; the client will respond right away and tell you that the check is on its way. That one time out of ten, things will not go so smoothly, and you'll have to do some conflict resolution.

There are two types of non-paying clients; clients who can't pay and clients who won't pay. For a client who won't (or doesn't want to) pay, the typical non-payment situation arises at some point after you submit a translation. The client lets you know that your work was not of the quality they expected, and because of this the client incurred unexpected costs. For example the client may tell you that they had to have the project re-translated entirely, or that your work required more editing than they had budgeted for, etc. Ideally the client should give you the chance to correct your errors and be paid the full amount you agreed on, but the project's deadline may not allow for this. The client may ask you to discount your rate of payment in order to make up for the extra cost of editing or re-translating your work.

If or when this happens, it is truly horrible and painful to have your translation skills criticized. However, it's important to remember that the client is already anxious and angry; denying that any problem could have existed will probably only make the situation worse. Before you try to defend yourself, make sure that you followed the client's instructions to the letter. If the client provided a list of terms, make sure that you used them. If the client asked you to format the translation as closely as possible to the original document, make sure that you did this. If the client asked for the document in a certain font, make sure that you used it. If you are completely convinced that you completed the translation to the client's specifications, ask to see a copy of the edited or re-translated translation so that you can see your real or perceived errors. Then, decide if you think that the client's claim is valid or not. In some cases, this may require going to a third party, such as another translator selected by you or the client, to make a decision as to whether the translation is high quality or not. Although it is sometimes painful to do this, it's important to acknowledge that there is some possibility that the client may be right and that you did an unsatisfactory job; insisting otherwise will probably not lead to a satisfactory outcome for you.

How much you press the quality issue with the client depends partially on how big the project is. If your fee for the project is only $50.00, it probably isn't worth arguing with the client over whether you did a satisfactory job; with the time it would take to go over the revised translation, submit a list of points that you disagree with, etc., you're probably better off simply letting go of the $50.00. If the project is $5,000 and the client is refusing to pay, it's a different story. As of this writing, there is no industry standard dispute arbitration process for translation; for example the American Translators Association does not intervene in disputes between translators and their clients, so it's up to you as an individual to work things out.

The second type of non-paying client, the client who can't pay, presents more of a problem. This type of client may start out with excuses that seem reasonable: accountant is on vacation, payment will be made by a certain date, large client is late on paying your client, invoice was lost/never received/sent to the wrong person/accidentally deleted, etc., but soon these explanations will prove to be untrue. The client may come out and admit that they are having cash flow problems, or may string you along indefinitely, or go out of business and/or file for bankruptcy. The first step with this type of non-paying client is to send a series of three to four increasingly serious reminder letters, known formally as *dunning letters*. You can start out by politely reminding the client of the terms you agreed on and asking them to pay, then escalate the situation to include copies of the letter to higher-ups at the agency or company, then finally threatening to involve a third party. This third-party involvement may be in the form of taking the client to small claims court, hiring a third-party collection agency, or contacting the end client for the translation and letting them know that you were never paid for your work, and that because of this, they may be violating United States copyright law by using your translation. If you send this type of letter, it is very important to consult a lawyer or at least familiarize yourself with the legal requirements in order to make sure that you are not breaking the law by saying something untrue or misleading. Following are some examples of first, second and final notice dunning letters.

Sample First Notice

Dear *Name of Person who assigned you the project*:

According to my records, I have not received a check for Invoice #_____ for _____ which was due for payment on _____. Please let me know the status of this payment at your earliest convenience, and thank you again for your business.

Sample Second Notice

Dear *Name of Person who assigned you the project (CC to this person's Accounts Payable Department or Supervisor)*:

I recently contacted you regarding an overdue payment for Invoice #_____ for _____ which was due for payment on_____. As of today I have not received this payment, and I do need to hear from you regarding its status, as the payment is now considerably past due. Please reply to me as soon as possible and let me know the date on which you will be mailing this payment, if it has not already been sent.

Sample Final Notice

Dear *Name of Person who assigned you the project (CC to this person's Accounts Payable Department or Supervisor)*:

Despite my two previous notices to you on _____ and _____, I have not yet received your overdue payment for Invoice #_____ in the amount of _____. Please understand that you have had sufficient time and notice regarding the status of this payment. Failure on your part to pay this seriously overdue invoice by _____ may result in my posting information about this transaction to translation industry payment practices lists, referring this account to a third party collection agency, and/or contacting the end client of the translation in question to inform them of the non-payment situation. I trust this will not be necessary, and look forward to receiving your payment as soon as possible.

If you need to involve a third-party collection agency and you are an ATA member, you can investigate the services of ATA's affiliate program with Dunn and Bradstreet Receivables Management. They handle both U.S. and international unpaid accounts, and normally take 25–50% of what they collect. Other third-party collection agencies exist, but make sure that the agency is legitimate before you hire them; for example call the Better Business Bureau where the agency is headquartered and find out if there have been any complaints against the agency.

If you get to the point of sending dunning letters to a client, there is unfortunately some possibility that you will never get paid in full. Many translators feel that if more than four months have elapsed since the original payment deadline, the client is probably not going to pay without some serious outside incentive to do so. Dunning letters can motivate a client who is either trying to delay payment, or trying to see who complains most loudly about not getting paid. However, if the client absolutely doesn't have the money to pay you or goes bankrupt, there may not be much you can do if your dunning letters don't get a response; further proof that you're much better off investigating the client up front than fighting for months to get your payment after the fact.

4.8.1 Arbitration and dispute resolution

Another avenue to pursue with a non-paying client is arbitration, a non-court proceeding involving an independent and neutral arbitrator. Arbitrators are often attorneys, and you may choose to have your own attorney represent you during arbitration. One important element of arbitration is that unlike filing in small claims court, you normally cannot file for arbitration without the cooperation of your non-paying client, since they are usually required to fill out the arbitration submission agreement along with you. For more information, see the website of the American Arbitration Association http://www.adr.org .

4.9 Cash flow issues

Happily most translators go for long periods of time without ever dealing with a non-paying client. The larger and more common problem is clients who don't pay on time. Some clients only issue checks on certain days of the week or month, so if you contact them on June 10 to let them know that the payment due June 1 didn't arrive, they may not be able to issue a check until June 15. With the time needed to mail the check, you might receive this payment three weeks late.

It's up to you as a freelancer to decide how to deal with cash flow issues. When you have a full-time job, it's a pretty safe bet that your paycheck that's due on the 25th will be in your account in time to pay your mortgage on the 1st, but a freelancer would be unwise to take this kind of gamble. This is an important issue to consider before you start working as a freelancer. If you are planning on translation being your primary source of income, make sure that you have enough of a cash cushion that you're not left scrambling when a check doesn't arrive as planned.

5 Setting up your business for growth

When you're putting together your first translation résumé and wondering who your first clients will be, it's hard to imagine the day when you'll be turning down work, or kept consistently busy by a slate of regular clients. In today's translation climate where many translators have never been busier, it's important to look a year or two down the road and see where you'd like to be and how to set your business up to get there.

One of the most important steps you can take at the start of your business is to log all of the business contacts you make in an organized format. Over the course of your first year in business, if you market yourself aggressively, you will probably have contact with 300 or more potential clients. Rather than counting on your memory to remind you who these people are, or deleting their "thanks, but no thanks" e-mails, you can save and organize their contact information in order to make use of it later. There are various ways to do this; on paper, using an index card file; or electronically, using a spreadsheet or more sophisticated contact management software. The key element is to keep track of the name of the person you e-mailed or spoke with, all of his or her contact details, and a reminder about what you communicated about. This way, if a potential client tells you, "We only work with translators who have more than three years' experience," you can contact them again when you meet their requirement. If a potential client tells you that they're not taking applications in your language pair right now, contact them again in six months to a year to let them know you're still interested. You can also use this list of contacts to build a mailing list for your own e-newsletter or other promotional tools.

Setting up a semi-automated invoicing system is another way to set your business up to grow. Once you're working steadily, billing takes a great deal of time if you do it manually, since a busy translator could generate 100 or more individual invoices during a year. Here you have several options such as using accounting software that includes an invoicing tool or setting up an invoicing system using a spreadsheet program such as OpenOffice.org Calc. Whatever option you choose will take some time to set up initially, but will save time when you don't need to enter a client's contact and billing information manually on every invoice.

If you're looking for even more office automation, you can use a company such as MyBizOffice http://mybizoffice.com or others that will bill your clients for you, deduct taxes from what you make, and funnel money into a 401K plan. Most of these services, also called *umbrella companies* or *employers of record*, charge about 5% of your gross income. If you are incorporated, you can also hire an accountant to process your payroll for you and calculate the amount you owe in taxes.

Even if you're not interested in running a translation agency, another step toward scaling up is to find other translators in your language combinations and specializations with whom you can share work. Especially if you would like to work for direct clients, it can be a big asset to offer a team of two or three translators if the client needs fast turnaround on a large project. Your local ATA chapter and the annual ATA conference are an excellent resource for meeting people like this.

5.1 Incorporating and planning for taxes

Some translators operate their businesses as sole proprietors for many years, while others incorporate immediately. It's a good idea to talk to an accountant about whether incorporating would be a good idea for you. While the best option here is to contact a qualified accountant or small business consultant, following is an overview of some of the advantages and disadvantages of incorporating:

Separation of finances. Incorporating forces you to keep your business and personal finances separate, since your clients pay the corporation and then the corporation pays you wages, even if you're the only employee. In this way you are always sure how much the business is earning and how much you're spending on the business. However, as a sole proprietor you can achieve the same effect by having a business bank account and a personal one and carefully tracking how money flows between the two.

Limitation of liability. Since a corporation is its own legal entity, incorporating gives you some protection against personal liability. In most cases, your personal assets cannot be seized to pay the corporation's debts or legal judgments. If you are planning to work for direct clients or subcontract work to other translators, this alone can be a good motivation for incorporating.

Tax relief. Some corporate structures, such as *S corporations*, can save you money on taxes, since an S-corporation's profit is not subject to self-employment tax. Incorporating may also allow you to take more tax deductions than you do as a sole proprietor.

Capital. If you need to raise capital, for instance by taking out a business loan, it is often easier to do so if you are incorporated. However, so few translators take out business loans that this is not a major concern.

Expense. Depending on where you live, setting up a corporation may be extremely inexpensive or very expensive. For example, in some states it costs as little as 99 cents to file your articles of incorporation on-line, while in other states the fee may be much higher. Likewise, some states will require corporations to pay a filing fee for their required annual report, while others will not. Incorporating can also result in higher accounting expenses, since some corporation types must file payroll taxes every quarter.

Paperwork. Incorporating definitely requires extra paperwork. At the very least, you have to file *Articles of Incorporation* in your state, probably file a *Trade Name Registration* in your state and receive a *Federal Employer Identification Number* that you provide to clients instead of your personal Social Security number. If you hate doing accounting and don't want to hire someone to do it for you, this is definitely a consideration!

5.1.1 Corporate Entities

If you would like to incorporate, there are various corporate structures to choose from, such as an *S corporation*, *C corporation*, or *limited liability corporation* (LLC). Before incorporating, it is important to talk with an accountant or small business consultant about selecting the entity type that is right for you in your state; following is an overview of the most common entity types chosen by freelance translators.

C-corporation

Many large businesses are C-corps, but small businesses can choose this structure as well. One of the major advantages of a C-corp is that it allows you to deduct 100% of your health insurance premiums as a business expense. C-corp profits below $50,000 are also taxed at a lower rate than a comparable amount of taxable income.

S-corporation

This is possibly the most popular structure for a one-person corporation. The main advantage of an S-corporation is that as long as you pay yourself a "reasonable wage" (as defined by the IRS), you can pass some of the corporation's income on to your individual tax return, which can avoid you having to pay self-employment tax on it. For example if you have net income of $60,000 and pay yourself wages of $30,000 (which are subject to self-employment tax), you can then pass the additional $30,000 on to your individual tax return as profit, where it is subject only to regular income tax, not self-employment tax. One disadvantage of an S-corp is that all shareholders must be U.S. citizens or permanent residents; nonresident aliens cannot be S-corp shareholders.

Limited Liability Corporation

The "Single Member LLC" is probably the second most popular corporate structure for freelance translators. Like an S-corp, an LLC is a flow-through entity, allowing you to pass profits and losses on to your personal tax return. In addition, LLC owners may be nonresident aliens. In some states, LLCs have a limited duration, for example 30 years or less, so if you are incorporating early in your career, be sure to investigate this in your state.

Sole Proprietor

A self-employed person whose business is not incorporated is referred to as a sole proprietor. Being a sole proprietor has its advantages, including very little administrative overhead. In many states you do not even need a business license to operate as a sole proprietor, and all of your income is simply reported on Schedule C of your individual tax return. However as a sole proprietor, you have no liability protection in the event of a lawsuit or financial claim (meaning that at least in theory, your personal assets can be seized), and all of your income is subject to self-employment tax.

5.1.2 Tax planning

Whether you incorporate or not, tax planning is a crucial element of being self-employed, and one that catches many people by surprise. When you have a full-time job, you accept the fact that some of your salary goes to taxes, but you usually don't have to write out a check to the federal or state government for that amount. As a freelancer, you will be responsible for tracking and paying your taxes, normally done four times a year. If you are incorporated, you will probably have to pay payroll taxes, and if you are a sole proprietor you will probably have to file estimated taxes every quarter to avoid owing a large amount plus penalties at the end of the year.

The most important element of paying your own taxes is to meticulously keep track of your income and expenses. Whether you do this on your computer or on paper, it is imperative to write down the date and amount of every payment you receive and every purchase you make for your business, and to save all receipts. The amount of tax you will pay depends of course on how much you earn and your overall tax situation, but it is important to factor the additional tax you pay as a self-employed person into your projections. The self-employment tax, currently 15.3% of your net earnings from self-employment, consists of 12.4% of your income for Social Security, up to a maximum of $10,788, and 2.9% of your income for Medicare. The reason these taxes can come as a shock is that when you have a full-time job, your employer pays half of these taxes and you pay half; but when you're self-employed, you pay the entire amount. Also keep in mind that you pay the self-employment tax *in addition* to regular income tax, not instead of it, so for most freelancers, this will mean allocating approximately 40% of your income for taxes.

On the up side, as a self-employed person you have many more opportunities than your salaried friends to reduce your tax burden through deductible business expenses. Here again, it's important to talk to an accountant or tax preparer to find out what is deductible in your particular situation. However, most self-employed translators can deduct home office expenses, computer hardware and software, Internet and phone costs, travel expenses, professional association memberships, continuing education, office supplies, business-related travel, professional journal subscriptions, books, dictionaries, even meals out that are work-related. Following is an overview of the basic entity types to consider; but note that these business entities are regulated in the U.S. by individual states rather than at the federal level, so be sure to research the laws of the state you live in.

5.2 Key Questions Before the Project Starts

Landing your first few clients will be one of the most exciting experiences of your freelance career; after all of your hard work planning and preparing, the day will come when a client will offer you a real live paying translation job, and it's incredibly exciting. At the same time, it's important to keep a level head and realize that being offered the project doesn't mean that you just say "Yes," without even knowing what the work consists of. Sometimes, saying "No" can be a better decision for your career in the long run. It is critical to remember that it takes a lot of hard work to build a good reputation, and just one poorly done project to spoil that reputation.

Before accepting a project, ask yourself...

- *Am I comfortable with the subject matter?* Along with failing to investigate a potential client's trustworthiness, this is probably the biggest mistake made by beginning translators. If you don't know the difference between AC and DC power or what a solenoid is or how to change a spark plug, you'll be even more lost when trying to understand these items in one of your source languages. At the start, stick to material you feel very comfortable with. If you'd like to branch out into a more technical specialization, take some courses on the topic in your native language, and consider paying a translator who is experienced in that particular specialization to edit your work until you feel confident in your skills.

- *Can I finish this translation on time?* Tight deadlines are the reality of the modern business world, but you have to train yourself to recognize the difference between tight and impossible. 2,500 words due tomorrow is a tight deadline; 10,000 words due tomorrow is an impossible deadline. For a tight deadline, it's fair to charge a higher rate to make up for the fact that you have to work overtime; for an impossible deadline, the only course of action that will preserve the quality of your work is to say "No!"

- *Am I confident that this client will pay me?* If the client has a good track record of payment, the chances are that your money will come through. If the client is not an established business, it's up to you to judge and deal with the consequences. Just as you will be asking clients to take a chance on you as a new translator, you may need to take chances on your clients, but make sure to follow the steps previously discussed for investigating your clients before you work for them. Get full contact information and a written guarantee of payment before you start working.

- *Am I getting paid fairly for my work?* As a new translator, some of your prospective clients will be low paying, and this doesn't make them bad clients. Still, working for impossibly low rates devalues your own work and the work of other professional translators. If you agree to work for less than your usual rate, it should be for a good reason, for example the client is a non-profit organization, or the project is very large and has a flexible deadline.

Before accepting a project, ask the client some or all of the following questions. For small jobs from regular clients, you may not have to go through the entire list, and clients who have done their homework will often volunteer the answers to these questions before you ask.

- *What type of document is this?* What format is the document in (hard copy, hand written, PDF, Word, Excel, HTML, etc.)?

- *What is the subject matter?*

- *How many words or pages is the document?*

- *What is the deadline?* Once you've asked this, make sure that you can make the deadline!

- *May I see a sample of the document before accepting the project?* This is always a good idea, and even if the material is highly confidential, the client should be able to e-mail or fax you something like the table of contents or the index. Seeing a sample helps you decide how long the translation will take—is it 20 pages of barely legible handwriting, or 20 pages of neatly typed copy? Does the document contain complex formatting that will have to be reproduced?

- *What will the translation be used for?* You need to know if the advertising text they're sending you is intended as a "for information only" document for their sales team, or to be published in a highly visible place. This is a critical question that many translators skip.

- *What format should I deliver the translation in?* You need to know what file format the client wants; in some rare cases the client may also want a faxed or mailed hard copy.

- *Should I reproduce the formatting of the source document?* In most cases, clients will want the translation to look as much as possible like the source document. Sometimes, they just want to know what the documents say, so the formatting doesn't matter.

- *Who will answer my questions about this translation?* Many beginning translators are afraid that asking questions will make them seem unequal to the task at hand. On the contrary, it's important that if you don't understand what a term means and can't find the answer in any of your usual resources, you don't just guess and hope that no one will notice. The client should tell you up front who will answer your questions and how to submit them.

- *My rate for this translation would be...* It is absolutely critical to settle the question of rates and payment terms before you accept any translation work. Make sure that you agree on a per word rate, and whether the rate is charged on the source or target word count; in some cases the rate will be hourly. Then, clarify what the client's payment terms are, and if the payment is not by check or direct deposit, clarify who is paying for costs such as wire transfer or credit card fees (normally the client pays their fees and you pay yours, but if you don't specify, some clients will deduct their bank fees from your payment). Some clients will tell you what they're willing to pay for a specific project, but most will ask what you'll charge. The first time this happens is incredibly anxiety-provoking, as you have only a few seconds to come up with a price that isn't insanely high or low. If you've done your own homework and made a rate sheet in advance, your nerves will be considerably calmer when you get to the point of discussing rates.

- *Please send me a purchase order, contract, or written confirmation of the guidelines for this project.* If the client is not a regular one, it's important to have some written evidence of your business agreement with them. Without this, it's your word against theirs as to what terms you agreed on.

5.3 How to Raise Your Rates

At some point in your translation career, you'll realize that your translation experience or specializations can command higher rates than what you're currently charging. Also, you might be interested in either earning more money or in working less, so you might need to charge more at some point.

Unfortunately, the answer to the question, "How do I get my existing clients to pay me more money?" is almost always, "You can't." Most often, the best way to raise your rates is to look for new, higher paying clients. For example, if you've worked for a translation agency for two years, making 12 cents a word, your client might be willing to go along with a rate increase to 14 cents a word, but it's highly unlikely they'll agree to pay 25 cents a word. In some easily outsourced language pairs such as English into Spanish, there may even be pressure on translators to decrease their rates over time. On the other hand, if you land a direct client who is used to paying 30 cents a word for translation through an agency, your offer of 25 cents a word may strike them as the best deal they've gotten all year. You simply have to eliminate your lowest paying clients and look for higher paying ones to replace them.

One of the best strategies for raising your rates is to look for clients who themselves earn a healthy income, or orient yourself toward higher-earning specializations. Not surprisingly, business sectors that are big earners in the U.S., such as law, financial services and pharmaceuticals, are correspondingly well-paying for translators who work in those areas. So, part of the key to raising your rates is to find clients who can pay what you'd like to earn, and show these clients that your services will help their businesses run faster, more effectively or more profitably.

5.4 Ten ways to please a translation client

The easiest way to keep your translation business profitable is to cultivate a core group of regular clients who will fill your in-box with translation projects, allowing you to spend your time working rather than looking for work. Implementing some of the tips below will help you keep a regular stream of work coming your way.

1. **Meet every deadline.** If you can't consistently meet deadlines, you're not well-suited to being a freelance translator. Remember that your clients have deadlines too, and are sometimes waiting for your work as part of a larger project. As one experienced translator comments, "8:00 means 7:50, not 8:10."

2. **Be easy to reach.** Put your contact information in your e-mail signature file, so that a client never has to look up your phone or fax number. Realize that many times, if clients cannot reach you immediately, they will contact another translator. Since over 90% of contacts from clients will be by e-mail, put an auto-responder on your e-mail if you will be out of the office for even a few hours.

3. **Follow directions.** While it can be time-consuming to follow many different clients' particular ways of doing things,

you will save the client time and money, and thus get more work from them, by following their instructions to the letter. If the client asks you to put your initials in the file name, do it. If the client asks you to put the word "Invoice" in the subject line of the e-mail containing your invoice, do it.

4. **Don't waste your clients' time.** It's acceptable, and even encouraged to ask questions when you need to clarify something. However, it's also important to show respect for your clients' time, and for the fact that yours is probably not the only project they are handling. Keep your e-mails short and to the point, and make your questions clear and easy to answer.

5. **Provide referrals.** Many translators worry that providing referrals to other translators in the same language combination will lead to less work for themselves, but in fact the opposite seems to be true. Clients like to work with freelancers who solve the clients' problems, and when you're too busy and can't handle their work or are going on vacation, it's a problem for them. Have the names of two or three translators in your language combination who you really trust, and provide these names to your clients when you aren't available for work.

6. **Be easy to work with.** This isn't to say that you should be a pushover or let clients take advantage of you, but for your regular clients, it's worth putting in some extra effort. Thank them for giving you their business; be friendly and polite if a payment is unexpectedly late; fill in for them in a pinch when another translator lets them down.

7. **Ask for constructive criticism.** It's important to see feedback as part of your quality assurance process, not as an attack on your abilities as a translator. If a client asks for changes in your translation, make them politely and immediately; if you decide later that the changes are unnecessary and you don't want to work for the client again, it's another matter. With your regular and trusted clients, periodically

ask what you can do to better meet their needs, then implement these changes.

8. **Appreciate your clients.** Your regular clients are the people who make it possible for you to earn a healthy income while living a flexible and self-directed freelance lifestyle. A small gift at the end of the year is always appreciated when a client has given you regular work.

9. **Don't bicker.** If a prospective client offers you a project at a ridiculously low rate, politely decline it, possibly sending them a copy of your standard rate sheet if you have one. Don't insult them for offering such low pay or make negative comments about their business; just courteously decline to work for them and let them move on to someone else.

10. **Charge what you're worth, and earn it.** There will always be another translator out there who is willing to work for one cent per word less than you are, so don't compete on price alone. Giving your clients a little more effort than necessary proves to them that often, they get the level of service they pay for.

Resources

U.S. Government agencies employing translators and interpreters

Central Intelligence Agency

The CIA http://cia.gov offers a number of opportunities such as Foreign Language Instructor, Language Specialist, Foreign Media Analyst and National Clandestine Service Language Officer. Requirements and salaries vary, but most positions are full-time and the largest number of opportunities is in the Washington, DC area. Applicants must be U.S. citizens and willing to complete a medical and psychological exam, polygraph interview and background investigation.

Federal Bureau of Investigation

The FBI http://fbi.gov offers salaried Language Analyst positions as well as full-time or part-time Contract Linguist positions. Positions are located at the FBI's Washington, DC headquarters or at regional Field Offices. Applicants must be U.S. citizens and willing to complete a polygraph interview and background check. Language Analyst applicants must be willing to travel on temporary assignments for 30 days at a time.

State Department Office of Language Services

The State Department http://state.gov employs staff translators and interpreters and maintains a roster of freelance translators and interpreters. Application is by competitive examination; interpreter candidates must be willing to travel internationally for at least three weeks at a time.

National Security Agency

The NSA `http://www.nsa.gov` is especially interested in hiring Language Analysts for Asian and Middle Eastern languages, but employs translators and interpreters in a variety of languages. The NSA also administers the Language Enhancement Program, which re-trains French, German, Italian, Portuguese, Russian or Spanish linguists to work in Asian and Middle Eastern languages.

Associations for translators and interpreters

American Translators Association

The ATA `http://atanet.org` is the largest association of translators and interpreters in the U.S.; offers its own translator certification exam to members, publishes the monthly *ATA Chronicle*, and organizes a wide range of professional development activities including an annual conference. The ATA website also lists numerous local ATA chapters.

National Association of Judiciary Interpreters and Translators

NAJIT `http://najit.org` is a professional association for court interpreters and legal translators. Publishes a quarterly journal, *Proteus*, and organizes an annual conference. Website includes helpful information about the court interpreting profession.

Translators and Interpreters Guild

TTIG `http://ttig.org` is the only nationwide labor union of translators and interpreters. Offers a translator and interpreter referral service as well as other membership benefits in cooperation with the Newspaper Guild–Communications Workers of America.

American Literary Translators Association

The American Literary Translators Association http://literarytranslators.org is a professional association for translators of literature in all languages. Publishes a newsletter and the *Translation Review*, website also includes a list of university-level literary translation programs.

International Association of Conference Interpreters

Membership in the AIIC http://aiic.net is open only to experienced conference interpreters who are sponsored by current AIIC members. However, website includes helpful information for those who would like to pursue conference interpreting opportunities.

Selected training programs and home study courses for translators and interpreters

In general, translator and interpreter training programs are not language courses, and applicants are expected to have a high degree of fluency in English and at least one other language before applying. Most colleges and universities and even some community colleges and adult continuing education programs offer foreign language skill development courses. For a list of translation degree and certificate programs that are approved by the American Translators Association to fulfill its education and experience requirement for translator certification candidates, visit the *Certification* section of atanet.org. For more information on translator and interpreter training programs, see the publication *Park's Guide to Translating and Interpreting Programs in North America*, published by the American Translators Association.

Monterey Institute for International Studies

Located in Monterey, California, Monterey Institute http://miis.edu offers graduate programs through its Fisher Graduate

School of International Business, Graduate School of International Policy Studies, Graduate School of Language and Educational Studies, and Graduate School of Translation and Interpretation, as well as intensive language courses. As of this writing, candidates for the two-year M.A. degree in Translation, Translation and Interpretation, or Conference Interpretation must have fluency in English and at least one of: Chinese, French, German, Japanese, Korean, Russian or Spanish.

Kent State University Institute for Applied Linguistics

Located in Kent, Ohio, the Institute for Applied Linguistics http://appling.kent.edu offers undergraduate and graduate translation degrees; a B.S. in Translation and an M.A. in Translation. Current language combinations offered by the program include English paired with French, German, Japanese, Russian or Spanish.

University of Hawaii at Manoa Center for Interpretation–Translation Studies

The CITS http://cits.hawaii.edu does not offer a degree program, but conducts a summer certificate program for translators and interpreters who work in English paired with Japanese, Mandarin Chinese or Korean. During the school year, the CITS offers a General Skills Training program for translators and interpreters.

Logos free online translation theory and practice courses

Logos http://logos.it, which is also a language services provider, offers two free self-paced translation courses on its website. One course covers general translation theory and practice, and one course covers literary translation. Although the courses do not provide any practice exercises or feedback, they are excellent starting points for beginning translators.

Bellevue Community College

Located in Bellevue, Washington, BCC `http://bcc.ctc.edu` offers the only translation and interpretation certificate programs in the Pacific Northwest. Language combinations depend on student demand, and students can take courses toward either a certificate program, or for continuing education.

Brigham Young University

Located in Provo, Utah, BYU `http://byu.edu` offers a B.A. degree in Spanish Translation.

Rutgers University Department of Spanish and Portuguese

Located in New Brunswick, New Jersey, Rutgers University `http://span-port.rutgers.edu` offers a Certificate of Proficiency in Spanish→English and English→Spanish translation, which may be taken on its own or in combination with an M.A degree in Spanish.

Southern California School of Interpretation

With campuses throughout California and Nevada, Southern California School of Interpretation `http://interpreting.com` specializes in short (4–11 week) courses to prepare students to take State and Federal interpreter certification exams.

ACEBO interpreter training products

ACEBO `http://acebo.com` offers the popular home study course *The Interpreter's Edge*, which helps court interpreters prepare for certification exams. The tape set is currently available in a generic (non-language specific) version, or for English paired with Spanish, Cantonese, Mandarin, Korean, Vietnamese, Polish, Russian, Japanese, Portuguese or Arabic.

Florida International University

Located in Miami, Florida, Florida International University http://w3.fiu.edu/translation offers a certificate in Spanish↔English translation studies and a certificate in Spanish↔English legal translation and court interpreting.

Binghamton University Translation Research and Instruction Program

Located in Binghamton, New York, this campus of the State University of New York http://trip.binghamton.edu offers a certificate in translation, an M.A. in comparative literature with a concentration in literary translation, and a Ph.D. in translation studies.

The Graduate School of the College of Charleston

Located in Charleston, South Carolina, the Bilingual Legal Interpreting Program http://cofc.edu (not offered during the 2006–2007 school year) offers both a Master's degree and a certificate program in Spanish↔English bilingual legal interpreting.

American University

American University http://american.edu, located in Washington, DC, offers certificate programs in French, Russian and Spanish translation.

New York University School of Continuing and Professional Studies

With both on-site (New York, New York) and online courses, NYU http://scps.nyu.edu offers a certificate in Arabic, French, German, Spanish or Portuguese translation, paired with English. Courses that are offered online only include German→English, English→Portuguese and Arabic→English.

The National Center for Interpretation at the University of Arizona

Located in Tucson, Arizona, NCI `http://nci.arizona.edu` offers training for Spanish court and medical interpreters, and through its Agnese Haury Institute for Court Interpretation, offers a three-week intensive Spanish↔English court interpreter training program every summer.

University of Wisconsin at Milwaukee

UWM `http://uwm.edu` offers both an M.A. and a graduate certificate in French, German and Spanish translation.

The University of Geneva School of Translation and Interpreting

Known worldwide for training high-level translators and conference interpreters, the ETI `http://unige.ch/eti` (School of Translation and Interpreting), located in Geneva, Switzerland, offers programs in German, English, Arabic, Spanish, French, Italian and Russian translation at the undergraduate, graduate and certificate levels.

Middlebury College Language School

In business for nearly 100 years, the Middlebury College Language School `http://middlebury.edu/academics/ls`, located in Middlebury, Vermont, is not specifically geared toward translation, but offers intensive summer classes in Arabic, Chinese, French, German, Italian, Japanese, Portuguese, Russian and Spanish. Students must commit to speaking only their target language for the duration of the program, and the Language School also offers graduate programs overseas.

Glossary

American Translators Association
: *Known by its initials, ATA, the largest organization for translators and interpreters in the United States.*

alignment
: *The process of pairing source and target documents to create a database of bilingual sentence pairs.*

back-translation
: *A translation of a translation, translating the target text back into the source language.*

bilingual
: *In the translation industry, a term often used for a person who is a native speaker of two languages.*

CAT tool
: *Computer-assisted translation tool; a piece of software that helps a human translator work faster and more consistently be recycling previously translated material. Also referred to as a translation memory tool or translation environment tool.*

certified translator
: *Normally, a translator who has passed the American Translators Association certification exam, although this designation is sometimes used for various other credentials, such as having completed a translation certificate program.*

cleaned file
: *A file containing only the target language text, with the source text and translation memory program codes removed.*

computer-assisted translation tool	*Often referred to as* CAT *tools, this software, under ideal circumstances, helps a human translator work faster and more consistently by recycling text that has already been translated and suggesting possible matches with text to be translated.*
dominant language	*The language in which a person is most comfortable speaking or writing. This may be the person's native language, or, in the case of a person educated primarily in a country where his/her native language is not spoken, may be different from the native language.*
EOM	*End of month, often used in combination with payment terms such as* 30 days EOM, *meaning that the translator will be paid within 30 days from the end of the month in which an invoice is issued.*
FIGS	*French, Italian, German and Spanish, the most commonly translated languages in the United States.*
heritage speaker	*In the U.S., a person who learned a non-English language by being exposed to it at home.*
interpreter	*A person who has a high degree of knowledge in two or more languages and changes spoken words from one language to another.*
invoice	*A statement from a translator to the translation client or translation agency, listing the services the translator performed and the amount that is owed for the services*
language pair	*The two languages in which a translator works.*
literary translator	*A translator who works with novels, stories, poems or plays.*

localization | *The process of adapting a product, piece of software or text document for use in another target market. This may involve translation, converting units of measurement, adapting graphics and other processes.*

machine translation | *Translation done by a computer.*

Net 30 | *The most common payment terms in the U.S., meaning that the translator will be paid within 30 days of an invoice being issued.*

native language | *A person's first language, which may also be the person's dominant language, or, in the case of a person educated in a country where their native language is not spoken, may be different from the dominant language.*

non-compete agreement | *An agreement stating that a translator will not seek business from a translation agency's clients for a certain period of time.*

non-disclosure agreement | *Often referred to as an NDA, an agreement stating that a translator will keep certain pieces of information confidential.*

passive bilingual | *A person who has excellent comprehension of a language, but speaks or writes the language poorly. Many heritage speakers are passively bilingual.*

per-word rate | *The amount of money that a translator is paid for each word translated.*

project manager | *A person who coordinates the administrative aspects of a translation or localization project.*

register | *The level of formality or informality in a piece of writing or speech. A translated document should be written in the same register as the source document.*

source language	*The language from which a translation is done.*
source text	*The text from which a translation is done.*
specialization	*A subject area in which a translator has in-depth knowledge; for example a former accountant might specialize in financial translation.*
TMX	*Translation Memory eXchange, an open standard for the exchange of translation memories.*
target language	*The language into which a translation is done.*
technical translator	*A translator who works with scientific, computer or engineering materials. Sometimes used to mean a non-literary translator, regardless of the translator's specializations.*
terms of service	*The conditions under which a translator or translation agency will provide services.*
translation agency	*A company serving as an intermediary between a translation client and a translator, often adding services such as project management, proofreading, and desktop publishing.*
translation memory tool	*Often used interchangeably with* computer-assisted translation tool, *a TM tool creates a database of previously translated text that can be used again.*
translation unit	*The "chunks" or segments into which a translation memory program or CAT tool breaks a source document; normally a translation unit is one sentence.*
translator	*A person who has a high degree of knowledge in two or more languages, and changes written documents from one language to another.*

Unicode

A standard system for the electronic representation of characters and symbols from all languages.

uncleaned file

A file containing the source and target translation units, along with the tags inserted by the translation memory program.

word count

The total number of words in a document, which may be based on either the source or target text, and may be calculated using a variety of methods.

XLIFF

eXtensible Localization Interchange File Format, an open standard for the exchange of localisation data.

Index

About the author

Corinne McKay is an American Translators Association-certified French to English translator specializing in legal, financial and marketing translations. After earning a B.A. and an M.A. in French and teaching high school French for eight years, she launched her home-based translation business and has never looked back! Based on her own experiences as a freelance translator, Corinne developed and teaches the popular online course *Getting Started as a Freelance Translator*, and has been selected as a presenter for the annual conference of the American Translators Association. She is a frequent contributor to translation industry publications, speaker for groups of aspiring translators and edits the e-newsletter *Open Source Update*, for translators interested in free and open source software. She lives in the foothills of the Rocky Mountains with her husband and daughter. Corinne can be contacted at books@translatewrite.com.

Colophon

This book was produced entirely with free/open source software running on Debian Gnu/Linux. The text was written in OpenOffice.org Writer and typeset with LyX using the KOMA-Script book class in the Palatino font. The cover was produced with Scribus and GIMP. The cover graphic is from an Illuminated Manuscript of the Arthurian Mythos from the Beinecke Rare Book and Manuscript Library, Yale University. The two panels portray King Henry requesting Walter Map to translate the Death of Arthur, and Arthur and his knights setting out for Winchester.

To order additional copies of **How to Succeed as a Free-lance Translator**, visit Translatewrite.com http://www.translatewrite.com.

For volume purchasing inquiries or to contact Corinne McKay about a media or speaking engagement, e-mail books@translatewrite.com or call 303-499-9622.

Hungry for more? Corinne McKay's online course *Getting Started as a Freelance Translator* builds on the concepts in this book and gives you six weeks of personalized coaching on starting your own home-based translation business. For more information or to register for the next session, visit Translatewrite.com http://www.translatewrite.com.